Doorways to Hope

Doorways to Hope

*Reflections on hope
for challenging times*

Christopher Chapman

CANTERBURY
PRESS

© Christopher Chapman 2025

First published in 2025 by the Canterbury Press Norwich

Editorial office
3rd Floor, Invicta House
110 Golden Lane,
London EC1Y 0TG, UK

www.canterburypress.co.uk

Canterbury Press is an imprint of Hymns Ancient & Modern Ltd
(a registered charity)

Hymns Ancient & Modern® is a registered trademark of
Hymns Ancient & Modern Ltd
13A Hellesdon Park Road, Norwich,
Norfolk NR6 5DR, UK

All rights reserved. No part of this publication may be reproduced,
stored in a retrieval system, or transmitted,
in any form or by any means, electronic, mechanical,
photocopying or otherwise, without the prior permission of
the publisher, Canterbury Press.

The Author has asserted his right under the Copyright, Designs and
Patents Act 1988 to be identified as the Author of this Work

Scripture quotations are from New Revised Standard Version Bible:
Anglicized Edition, copyright © 1989, 1995 National Council of the
Churches of Christ in the United States of America. Used by permission.
All rights reserved worldwide.

British Library Cataloguing in Publication data

A catalogue record for this book is available
from the British Library

ISBN: 978 1 78622 609 9

Typeset by Regent Typesetting

Contents

Acknowledgements ix
Introduction: What is hope? xi

The reflections

1. When things fall apart — 1
2. The many faces of hope — 4
3. Are you an optimist? — 7
4. The door of hope — 10
5. Listen to your longing — 13
6. Hope and her sisters — 16
7. Darkness, void and the breath of God — 19
8. God 'out there' or God 'here and now'? — 22
9. Resting in hope — 25
10. Treasures old and new — 28
11. Waiting — 31
12. Let's hear it for uncertainty! — 34
13. When there is no rain — 37
14. Turning 'buts' into 'ands' — 40
15. Hope's fabric — 43
16. The creative gaze of God — 46

17	In the valley of dry bones	49
18	Looking forward	52
19	Feeding the blackbirds	55
20	Remaking our mind maps	58
21	The dearest freshness deep down things	61
22	Hope and cooperation	64
23	Painting from your corner	67
24	God says: 'Go and have fun'	70
25	The heart in pilgrimage	73
26	Stepping into hope	76
27	Plodding on	79
28	Pilgrims of Hope	82
29	The crossroad	85
30	The grain of wheat	88
31	Comfort's root-room	91
32	Breaking the rules	94
33	Inclining the ear of the heart	97
34	The basket in the reeds	100
35	The opposition to hope	103
36	Hope and dialogue	106
37	Hope has two beautiful daughters	109
38	Swords into ploughshares	112
39	The woman with two coins	115
40	Easter hope wakes once more	118

Afterword   121

For Peter, Barbara and Patricia

Acknowledgements

I am grateful to Christine Smith and all at Canterbury Press for their openness to what I proposed and for their continued support.

I understand hope through those who have personified it for me. First among them is June, my wife, who continues to love me into being, with all the challenges this involves. My growth in hope also rests on the sensitivity and care shown to me by those who have accompanied me as spiritual directors over the years. Gratitude also goes to those with whom I have shared the work of hope at St Beuno's Jesuit Spirituality Centre; your friendship and example continue to enrich me. There are so many unnamed others who have sowed and nurtured the seed of hope in me. Thank you!

Introduction: What is hope?

These reflections explore the nature of hope, hope's roots in the activity of God, and ways of stepping into hope. These are challenging times when so much around us seems to be falling apart. We long for a brighter future, yet struggle to find reasons for hope. But then, what is hope? Is it wishful thinking: the desire to start or end anywhere other than where we are? Is it looking on the bright side, ignoring the presence of what is dark and difficult? Avoiding reality doesn't help us deal with it. Is hope a feeling? Yes – but is it only this? What happens when we are overwhelmed by a sense of hopelessness? Do we down tools and sit in the dust letting fate take its course? A fuller understanding of hope is needed if we are to engage creatively with the struggles and confusion within our daily experience and the harms we inflict upon the created world and one another. We need an understanding of hope that is grounded in what is real.

In these reflections I explore how hope has its roots in a God who is always moving into how things are. The door of hope is open and God steps through it with purpose and compassion. Through this same door we can step out in God into all that is broken apart. This is my own experience of working alongside people as a spiritual director and retreat giver. The hope that brings about change faces into, rather than avoids, what is real. This hope begins 'here' and 'now'. It is active, rather than passive. Yet, it is not enough to hope in God and fold our hands until the bad becomes good. Hope rests on our cooperation with its flow. In the face of violence and destructiveness, the biblical prophets saw that the work and the materials that went into making swords could better be used to make ploughshares. Someone has to begin melting down the metal and reshaping it in defiance of the wisdom of the warmongers. Hope is both the vision of what can be and the activity that realizes what is seen.

Pope Francis announced 'Pilgrims of Hope' as the guiding theme for the Catholic Church's life and work in 2025. In doing so he expresses what many of us feel deep down. We are at a pivotal point in human history and the history of our planet. To carry on as we are is to hasten our destruction. A difficult place requires a different response. Hope lies in daring a new path, away from attachment to control and possessiveness and towards relationships that honour one another and the created world. We are pilgrims of a future beyond our own.

The open door

> Look, I have set before you an open door, which no one is able to shut. (Revelation 3.8)

A closed door draws our attention; what's on the other side? Does it lead into a garden, a hidden room, or a cupboard full of treasures? It's hard to resist turning the handle to see what lies beyond. If the door is locked shut, we'll feel frustrated. But what if it is open? What might we discover? Hope is a door connecting what is now with a future we cannot yet see. The door is not bolted; we can open it and move through. In writing these reflections, my desire is to draw your attention to this door. It's there in the room where you are, even if it's not the place you planned to be in. You will need to approach the door and then step through. That might take some daring. You won't know what's there until you cross the threshold.

Linked together in a single passage within John's Gospel are two of the 'I am' sayings of Jesus: 'I am the good shepherd' and 'I am the door'[1] (John 10.1–11). One image is easy to visualize.

---

[1] The Greek word *thura* used here can mean door, gate or entranceway.

INTRODUCTION: WHAT IS HOPE?

We can see Jesus as one who leads and cares for those who are his, whatever the perils of the task might be. Likening a person to a gate or door asks more of our powers of imagination. The context within the passage helps. Through this door the shepherd's flock can move in and out and find pasture; it's an entranceway that leads to safe shelter and honours the freedom of those who pass through. While others come to 'steal and kill and destroy', Jesus' purpose is to share life in abundance. The presence of Jesus is a passageway from a restricted life to a liberated one. He is the door of hope that no one can shut. Fresh perspectives on hope come into view. Hope rests on God's longing and working for the good of all, rather than being dependent on our capacity to feel hopeful. Hope is about movement – a doorway we can choose to go through. The door is always open within the place where we are, for Jesus is God's I AM in the midst of all human experience.

Using the reflections

Whatever an author suggests, readers will read a book the way they want to. That's how it should be. Who am I to know what works best for you? But, that won't stop me making suggestions! Each reflection is relatively short. The inclination might be to turn the next page and read on. My sense is that it might be more fruitful to stay with what you have read and explore how it meets your experience; one line of thought might be enough for one day. We are used to travelling fast and being confronted with vast amounts of information. Views and news move through us without the time and space to absorb what we see or hear. The ancient monastic tradition of *lectio divina* invites the slow savouring of what we experience. What do you notice in the words you read? What thoughts or feelings are stirred up? How do these words resonate with your experience? Do you begin to sense some invitation within them? As you stay with what you have read, what settles within you as the day continues? To encourage this slow, soaking in of whatever is significant for you, I have provided some reflection and action exercises. If you are inclined to read through all the reflections in one go, pause now and then to notice what is connecting with you. Go back to a reflection that seemed significant. Stay with whatever is stirred up in you. Ask God to help you in this noticing and responding.

While each reflection is freestanding, I have arranged them with an order in mind:

- I begin by exploring the shape of hope from the perspective of the Christian tradition and how this compares with the different ways we use the word 'hope' within our everyday speech.
- I go on to look at how hope has its source in the God of hope. Is God 'out there' waiting for us to get our act together, or is God 'here' and 'now', working alongside us from the place where we are?
- The reflections then examine the relationship between hope and struggle. Our persistent experience is that we cannot wholly manage the course of events, or resolve our own difficulties unaided. As we look for mastery, we meet the challenge of mystery, and the God who meets us there.
- Hope is connected with vision, yet sometimes we do not see the way ahead. How might hope be at work for us when the road ahead is unknown and unseen?
- Hope connects with the way of pilgrims. The Holy Spirit in our spirit stirs us into movement. From confinement and fear, we are drawn into the wider horizons of faith, hope and love. Hope is a matter of choice and activity as much as feeling.
- Rather than passively waiting for things to change, we step into hope. No matter how great the challenges facing our time, hope invites us to do what belongs to us to do, and to trust that we are part of a larger story.

INTRODUCTION: WHAT IS HOPE?

Using the book with groups

While primarily arranged for individual reading, you can readily use this resource for groups, based around a weekly online or in-person meeting of about an hour. Here is one possible structure:

1 A time of informal gathering.
2 Opening prayer: this could be as simple as a short time of silence, followed by saying this quote from the letter to the Romans together:

> May the God of hope fill you with all joy and peace in believing, so that you may abound in hope by the power of the Holy Spirit. (Romans 15.13)

3 In turn, group members share one thing that has stayed with them from the reflections that week. Each offering is received respectfully, without discussion or comment, other than affirmation. A brief silence is held after each person's sharing.
4 When everyone who wishes to has contributed, the group spends two minutes in silence, letting God take them deeper into what has been shared.
5 There follows a second round of sharing: 'How has God spoken to us through what we have heard through one another?' Again, each offering is received respectfully, without discussion.
6 After these more structured times of sharing, you may want to include a space for open discussion and exploration of the themes that have emerged this week.
7 End the meeting with a time of prayer. This could be open prayer, flowing from the themes expressed across the session, or a time of silence followed by saying the quote from Romans 15 together.

1

When things fall apart

> O that you would tear open the heavens and come down …
> We all fade like a leaf,
>   and our iniquities, like the wind, take us away.
> There is no one who calls on your name,
>   or attempts to take hold of you;
> for you have hidden your face from us,
>   and have delivered us into the hand of our iniquity.
> Yet, O LORD, you are our Father;
>   we are the clay, and you are our potter;
>   we are all the work of your hand.
> (Isaiah 64.1, 6–8)

For humankind, these are difficult days. Many of us have the sense of living in a world that is falling part. Political life has tumbled into chaos. Trust in institutions is at a low ebb. Truth has so many versions and few we feel able to trust. Collectively, we seem to have taken a destructive lurch into division and the demonization of the other. Violence feeds further violence. The Earth goes on warming, fuelled by human indifference. We fade like a leaf; we fall into the hand of our own wrongdoing. Where are you, God, in all this? Have you hidden your face; or is it that we do not attempt to take hold of you? O that you would tear the heavens and come down!

It's not all bad news. Yesterday I heard about a woman who felt so concerned about the terrible conditions in which a friend lived that she galvanized her local community into working together to completely renovate her home. Formerly, the flat was dark, cold, damp and ridden with rats. Now, neighbours got together to renew walls, windows, flooring and heating – all at their own cost. A hell became a home, and the distress of a woman created community. Yet, even in this story so much remains ugly: why, for example, was this vulnerable person left helpless and isolated before her friend stepped in? I feel wonder at the generosity of volunteers who give their time freely in food banks to provide for those who would otherwise go hungry; but how have we come to such a place where the basic essentials for life remain out of reach for so many?

I can only watch so much news. I cannot live in constant view of the world falling apart. I need the simple joys of walking in the woods, reading a whodunnit, or being with friends to be able to look reality in the face. Yet it's important to let myself be disturbed by the hurt and harm we bring upon one another, and to see that I have a choice between being the cause of ills, or some part of their remedy. The more I reflect, the more I understand that what is happening in our time is the result of absence: the absence of respect and reverence for the other; the absence of justice and inclusion; the failure to recognize our interdependence with one another and with all that is created. It is the absence of what should be there that results in things falling apart, for bones need their sinews, bricks their mortar, leaves, light and warmth.

The medieval mystic, Julian of Norwich, was troubled by the struggles of the people of her time: prey to the worst effects of failing harvests, plague, war with France and the ruthless imposition of power by those in authority. She heard Jesus say, 'all will be well', but wondered how this could be so. If only God had done something to prevent the beginning of sin – by which she meant not only personal wrongdoing but the harms of her time – then all might be well; but as things were, how could all this hurt be healed? She struggled for many years to put together what didn't seem to fit: the God of love she believed in and the sufferings people endured. Amid her struggle one insight remained clear: if God was Being, and the source of all being, then human sin was nothing – that is, 'no-thing', the denial of being. For, sin, she wrote, has 'no kind of substance, no share in being; it is only known by the pain it causes'.[1] Sin is the absence of what connects people creatively and compassionately in patterns of shared flourishing. All falls apart through the lack of what should be there: no compassion, no honouring of the other, no justice. The leaf fades and the wind takes it away.

Yet God does not abandon us into the hands of our own wrongdoing; for God is the potter, still active and purposeful in working the clay. Even now, the God of hope is presence for absence, inviting us to share in shaping 'no-thing' into being.

For reflection and action

- Watch the news. Read the daily newspaper. What do you see reflected there about what causes the harm human beings do to one another and to the created world?
- Where do you see an opposite movement taking place, marked by compassion and creativity?
- Read and pray the lines from Isaiah that begin this reflection.

---

[1] Edmund Colledge and James Walsh, 1978, *Julian of Norwich: Showings*, translated and introduced by Edmund Colledge and James Walsh, New Jersey: Paulist Press, p. 148.

2

The many faces of hope

'Sir, you have no bucket, and the well is deep. Where do you get that living water? ...' Jesus said to her, 'Everyone who drinks of this water will be thirsty again, but those who drink of the water that I will give them will never be thirsty. The water that I will give will become in them a spring of water gushing up to eternal life.' (John 4.11, 13–14)

How many times have you used the word 'hope' in the last 24 hours? Setting out to write about hope, I notice how often it occurs in everyday conversation. Perhaps you will have voiced, or heard, sentences like these:

'I hope my next grandchild will be a boy.'
'I hope my train will be on time.'
'I am hopeful that things will turn out OK.'
'I hope you are well.'
'I hope I will live out my dream one day.'
'I hope it stops raining.'
'I hope for a better future for my children than the way things are now.'
'I hope you'll have a lovely holiday.'

Hope works in different ways within our speech. It can be a means whereby we send good wishes. During the worst of the Covid crisis, many emails began with a new greeting: 'I hope you are well.' Sometimes the word 'hope' carries our wish that events will turn our way: will our luck be in today? Beyond how events turn in a moment, hope can also express our deep and long-held desires, voicing our dreams and passions. Being 'hopeful' might reflect our optimistic disposition, should we have one.

Hope is a useful word; however, its very flexibility makes it difficult for us to know what is meant by Christian hope. I suspect we spend more time reflecting on the nature of love or faith than we do on hope, even though it too belongs as one of the three great virtues named by Paul in his letter to the Corinthians (1 Corinthians 13.13). Expressions of hope can seem flaky and passive in the face of the awfulness of war, oppression and poverty; wishful thinking just isn't enough. Even invoking the great window on hope provided by Jesus' rising from the dead can end up whitewashing the sustained suffering people endure. I have a painful memory of telling a long-time carer for his seriously ill wife how Christ's passion and resurrection made all things new, only for him to reply gently, 'Sometimes, it's difficult to understand.' Quick answers and slick theological formulae leave us feeling alone and empty.

If it is to be meaningful, hope has to be more than easy words and go beyond positive thinking. Hope must also transcend our capacity to *feel* hopeful, since this is so fragile in the face of difficulty, and hard to summon up in the experience of great harm. Hope has its source in God's enduring and purposeful presence and activity on our behalf. Words on their own are not enough. The Word takes on flesh. The God of hope chooses to be right there where you are and I am. The spring of hope is therefore beyond us; it is gift, rather than something we have to draw up from the deep by effort of will.

Hope is beyond us; and yet it is also within us. Jesus promised the woman at the well that a spring of living water would rise up inside her. She had to ask for what she lacked, and then trust and go with what was released in her. The woman who set out for the well in the heat of that day was dry and thirsty; her relationships had failed; men had ill-used her. She came alone, separated from the people of her village by their judgement of her, or her harsh verdict of herself. She returned to the village bubbling with energy, forgetful of her abandoned water jar, overflowing with the desire to share her experience. A spring had begun to flow within the unchanged circumstances of her life, and she was moving with it. She felt fresh, expansive life welling up through the narrow confines of her past experience. She sensed it was going somewhere new, without knowledge of where it would lead her. Hope is elusive like this, yet undeniably alive and purposeful. We cannot grasp water; the feeling of hope is not in our gift; but hope itself is given to those who seek it. The woman of the well gives a face to hope's indwelling and flowing. She invites us to go with her from wherever we begin, to wherever hope will lead us.

For reflection and action

- Today, notice how the word 'hope' is used in conversation.
- Can you sense hope welling up within you? If so, notice the direction of its flow and consider how to move with it.

3

Are you an optimist?

Always look on the bright side of life.[1]

Are you inclined to look on the bright side of life and to see the best in every situation? If so, perhaps you are an optimist. I am not an optimist. New Year celebrations have long found me out in that regard. I don't look forward with excitement and energy to what is to come in the months ahead. I have lived too long with doubt about my capacity to fulfil all that is expected of me to be free and easy about the future. Does that make me a pessimist? A friend who identifies himself as such explains that by anticipating the worst possible outcome, he is likely to be pleasantly surprised when disaster doesn't happen. I don't find it helpful to face into the future in that manner. If the worst comes, so be it; but I am resistant to welcoming the thought of it into every waking moment.

Both terms have Latin roots: optimism from *optimum*, meaning 'best', and pessimism from *pessimus*, meaning 'worst'. Yet, by and large, situations are neither best nor worst. In the grey zone of reality some of what we face is difficult and some holds future promise. What shapes our outlook is the way our feelings attach to one side above the other. For someone inclined to anxiety, fear will loom large, drawing them to look towards the obstacles in their path; for someone inclined to confidence, then the path itself shines with promise and the obstacles are hardly seen. Neither approach is capable of adequately evaluating the place where we are and how best to respond to it: pessimism can lead to paralysis; optimism to carelessness.

---

[1] Song title from Monty Python's *Life of Brian*, lyrics by Eric Idle.

How, for example, is humankind to respond to the challenge of global warming? We might conclude that collective agency on the scale necessary to make any meaningful reduction in the emission of greenhouse gases will remain lacking, whatever happens. On that basis it is useless to strive against the coming disaster. Or, we might be optimistic that humanity will find a technological solution to climate change, while glossing over the attitudes and behaviours that have fuelled the heating of our planet. Optimism is marked by freedom from fear of what is to come and confidence that things will work out. These are gifts that hold energy for positive forward movement. The danger of optimism is that in looking on the bright side it tends to ignore vital information on the darker edge of the situation. I might believe I can cross the road before the truck runs me down, but have I taken due account of its speed? This leads to one of the defining features of true hope. While hope, like optimism, looks to the future, it is rooted in a thorough engagement with the present. It faces into reality, not to be defeated or paralysed by it, but to take it fully into account in working for what is to come.

I wonder if I am being optimistic in growing tomatoes again this year. We have no greenhouse, so they must take their chance with the vagaries of the British summer. The last two years saw blight take hold and reduce the once promising looking fruit to mush. Tomatoes don't like humid, wet conditions; fungal infections do. I like home-grown tomatoes and there have been years when the yield has been good. Between putting in the plants and hoping for the best, and deciding blight will inevitably win and it's not worth the bother, there is a third option that I have gone with. I have planted the tomatoes in large pots against a sunny wall on the other side of the house from their usual station. I will water carefully, and remove lower branches to aid the flow of air. Optimism can err on the side of carelessness; pessimism on too easy acceptance of defeat. Hope learns from experience, explores possibilities, tackles issues, and pushes at doors that might open. In this sense, hope is less a feeling than a verb. 'I hope' becomes a statement of action rather than the expression of a good feeling in our bones.

Hope takes this very practical shape when we think about how to tackle global warming, how to build community in our neighbourhood, or how to respond to the personal challenges that face us. Hope is considered, imaginative and industrious. We start with a realistic assessment of how things are; we explore possible approaches; we do what we can. We are not alone in this. God's creativity works in this way too – through us if we allow it. The invitation to us is this: to set aside our natural inclination to optimism or pessimism, and to choose to be people of hope.

For reflection and action

- Hope learns from experience, explores possibilities, tackles issues, and pushes at doors that might open. Apply this approach to a challenge that faces you.
- Ask God for the gift of active hope.

4

The door of hope

> Therefore, I will now persuade her,
>   and bring her into the wilderness,
>   and speak tenderly to her.
> From there I will give her her vineyards,
>   and make the Valley of Achor a door of hope.
> (Hosea 2.14–15)

A door opened: we hesitated before stepping out of the dark room where we were confined, until the light beyond drew us out into the fresh air.

A door opened: someone came in to the room where we sat; we were no longer alone.

A door opened: we stepped into a situation we had hitherto avoided out of fear; it was time to act.

So much can change when a door opens. Perhaps you can remember moments when passing through a door created fresh movement in your life. Something ended then, and something began. In the Narnia chronicles, a wardrobe became a doorway to a different world. In the film *The Nun's Story*, Audrey Hepburn's character stepped through the convent door to join The Resistance. Open doors invite us into a new reality, a fresh possibility. A person we have not known steps through our door and a new relationship begins.

The book of Hosea hinges on the opening of a door of hope. Hosea tells of his unhappy relationship with his wife, Gomer. Gomer's history of unfaithfulness mirrors the failure of Judah and Israel to remain true to their covenant with God. Through his struggle between rejecting Gomer or taking her back, Hosea imagines the parallel conflict taking place in God. Will God reject Israel and turn away from Judah in return for their indifference to the ways of justice and loyalty? God proves unable to give them up to their fate. Despite everything, God's compassion grows warm and tender (Hosea 11.9). God will lead Israel out again into the wilderness where their relationship began; the Valley of Achor will become a door of hope.

The Valley of Achor – meaning 'the valley of trouble' – was an unlikely place for a new beginning; a site associated with greed and violence. A follower of Joshua, Achan, had taken gold and silver from the sack of Jericho, in direct defiance of the word of God. And there, at Achor, he was stoned to death (Joshua 7). It's a disturbing tale not only of human greed but of God's seeming inclination to violence. Is this how God is – answering human fallibility with the harshest of judgements? If so, there is no place for hope here. Yet Hosea sees God choosing Achor as the door through which hope will move. Hosea's children receive new names. Lo-ruhamah, 'the one who receives no pity', becomes the one on whom God has compassion. Lo-ammi, 'not my people', becomes 'you are my people' (Hosea 2.23). Presence for absence: 'no pity' becomes 'I will have compassion'; 'not my people' becomes the one who belongs. The valley of trouble becomes the door of hope, and this promise is made:

> I will take you for my wife for ever; I will take you for my wife in righteousness and in justice, in steadfast love, and in mercy. I will take you for my wife in faithfulness; and you shall know the LORD. (Hosea 2.19–20)

Hosea's struggle to comprehend the ways of God may reflect your own. Perhaps you wrestle with the question of who and how God is: the God of demand, harsh judgement and violence, or the God of steadfast love and mercy? Even now, there are those who invoke the name of God to back up their ruthless use of power and lack of pity. But it won't do, for as God says through Hosea, 'I am God and no mortal, the Holy One in your midst, and I will not come in wrath' (Hosea 11.9). The door opened, and mercy stepped through. Something ended, and a new reality began.

For reflection and action

- When has passing through a door created fresh movement in your life? Perhaps someone came in and a new chapter of your life began. Maybe you left something behind as you went through an open doorway; what began with that step out into a fresh space?
- When and how has God stepped into your life as if through an open door? Are there particular moments that stand out for you?
- Thinking about how life is for you now, is there a closed door that you feel drawn to open?
- Some words to ponder:

    'Listen! I am standing at the door, knocking; if you hear my voice and open the door, I will come in to you and eat with you, and you with me.' (Revelation 3.20)

5

Listen to your longing

O God, you are my God, I seek you,
  my soul thirsts for you;
my flesh faints for you,
  as in a dry and weary land where there is no water.
(Psalm 63.1)

For many years I have worked as a spiritual director. For those unfamiliar with the term, a spiritual director is one who accompanies another in listening to their experience and discerning what God's invitation to them at this time might be. That sentence begs a number of questions: How do we sense the work of God within our experience? How do we know it's God and not just our own imaginings? Is it correct to say that God 'invites'; isn't God about commandments and obedience? I won't be able to answer all these questions here – at least, not fully. What I can say is – through many hours of listening – that answers emerge from paying attention to your longing.

The word 'longing' deserves some pondering; it is 'long', suggesting a desire that is enduring, rather than an immediate 'want'. A longing reaches down to the depths of our being and stretches out towards our becoming. In this sense 'longing', when listened to, might give us clues about our true identity and how we are shaped to express this in our work and relationships. As we grow up, our understanding of who we are is influenced by how others respond to us. We work out how to meet the expectations of our immediate family. We learn how to survive in this environment. We pick up clues about how to be and what to do from the attitudes and behaviour of those around us. Together, these influences provide a mirror reflecting back who we are. All of this is normal, and generally for good. However, the mirror image we arrive at is limited. For example, I grew up well behaved and dutiful. At primary school the feedback on the Chapman children majored on their politeness and willingness to help. I picked up some tensions in the air at home and so determined to be a 'good boy', who worked out what other people needed him to be and tried to be that. I was in no way free and easy. Feelings were neatly tucked away since they weren't welcomed in polite conversation. I wasn't an angry person because anger was 'bad'. I didn't get too excited since restraint was the better way. To experience disapproval was my terror, and my limited experience of it haunted my dreams. Following these guidelines worked to a degree; but all I knew was the scaffolding of fitting in, not the building held within. And when the scaffolding began to fall apart from undue wear and tear, I was nothing.

Who we are is not only the sum of all we have inherited; it is also how we leave that inheritance and dare our own being. But how do we get to know who we are? Longing, in its varied expressions, provides some clues. One side of longing is recognizing what gives us energy. When do you feel alive? When are you able to be natural and free? These experiences might be rare. For most of the time we might stick with the familiar script we have been given or adopted. Feeling passionate, alive or joyful might have an element of surprise about it. Something deeper down of who we are is breaking through, wanting to be noticed. We might struggle to trust this energy; it doesn't fit comfortably with more familiar attitudes and patterns. Or perhaps these experiences are familiar but not fully welcomed, so we keep them tucked away, as if in a box in a rarely visited room. They don't fit with our received understanding of who we are or how to live.

Longing can be known by taking our wildest dreams more seriously. Is there something to be listened to within that wildness? What is it you want to do with your life? What could begin to move you in that direction? Longing can be recognized through paying attention to feelings we are likely to judge as negative: a persistent stirring of anger, frustration, boredom or sadness. What happens if we look on the underside of these feelings? What might they tell you about what you are not living out, or what you are not giving proper room for?

Longing reaches down to the depths of our being and stretches out towards our becoming. Being supported in listening to our longing helps us discover and befriend what lies within the scaffolding and, little by little, trust where this leads us. Hope is here, and we can taste it.

For reflection and action

Read Matthew 13.44–46, two parables that involve seeking and finding, and the daring leap that links them. What is your 'pearl of great price'? What will you give to find it? How will you seek for the buried treasure you hold within?

6

Hope and her sisters

And now faith, hope, and love abide, these three; and the greatest of these is love. (1 Corinthians 13.13)

Hope has two sisters: faith and love. Paul understands that there is an abiding familial bond between them. Faith, hope and love together express the life of God who is Trinity, One and Three. Like the Trinity, hope, faith and love can only take so much pulling apart. It's possible to describe hope alone, separate from her sisters; yet hope, like faith and love, is best understood within their trinitarian relationship.

All creation bears this relational imprint. We see the flow of water in a river through the light that falls upon it; and the beauty of light is revealed in its play with flowing water. We know the wind through the sway of leaves in a tall tree; and the tree's being is expressed as the wind passes through it. It is possible to study every living thing alone, but it is often better known and understood within relationship.

So it is that hope illumines faith, and faith, hope. Faith is not the summoning up of the feeling of certainty in relation to particular beliefs. That notion of faith is about being in control, with access to ready answers. Faith is almost the opposite; it's not about control, but that vulnerability that allows the growth of relationship. When I dare to trust another with who I am and what is important to me, I cannot know for certain that it is safe to do so or that it will turn out well. Yet without this vulnerability we will always remain distant. The daring of trust creates the room for closeness. Faith is this letting go into another's hands or stepping out in response to the other's invitation. Paradoxically, this vulnerable trust helps us know that it is ultimately safe to be vulnerable: this other will not let us fall or misuse our reliance on them. Faith in God has this shape. Hope, in conversation with faith, helps us go further. Trust in God in the moment is also cooperating with God in movement from 'what is' to 'what will be'. Abraham set out for a land he did not know in response to one who called him to do so (Genesis 12.1–4). Hope expresses that faith in God is dynamic and active: it is going somewhere; it is doing something.

Faith helps us understand that hope begins not by escaping reality but by trusting God's active presence within the complexity of how things are. Faith shows us that hope cannot exist separately from relationship with God; hope's movement has its source in rest in God. Hope expands through the experience of the faithfulness of God received through the daring of vulnerable trust.

Love brings light to hope, and hope to love. Hope reveals that love is always creative and purposeful; love works for transformation. Love's gaze sees not only what is but what will be. And hope for its part can only bear the shape of love. The orientation of hope is always compassionate; hope's vision and movement must serve relationships that honour the other, and build community. Hope for power, domination or self-aggrandizement is not hope. Without love, as Paul writes, we gain nothing and are nothing (1 Corinthians 13.1–3).

God is love; God is faithful; God is hope. These three sisters characterize the being and activity of God. As such they are traditionally described as theological virtues, for as we step into them, they draw us ever deeper within God. They help us know the life of God from the inside, by living in it. If over these pages you are led to reflect more deeply on the place of hope in your life, you will also find yourself learning more about faith and love.

The task of defining terms is an important one; without it our expression will lack clarity, and misunderstanding will follow. Yet, when it comes to the life of God, definition will have limits. I will fail to draw solid lines between faith, hope and love, and quite rightly so. That doesn't mean that nothing can be said; it's more that the something expressed will fall short. The inability to wholly separate faith, hope and love is also an invitation to wonder at the dance going on between them, like light upon the water and wind through the trees.

For reflection and action

Draw three overlapping circles – a 'Venn diagram' – one for faith, one for hope, one for love. Now, let words or images come to mind in relation to each circle, and place them wherever you sense they best belong.

7

Darkness, void and the breath of God

This is how the Bible begins:

> In the beginning when God created the heavens and the earth, the earth was a formless void and darkness covered the face of the deep, while a wind from God swept over the face of the waters. (Genesis 1.1–2)

Two brief verses express the many paradoxes within all the verses that will follow. In the beginning there is absence of form and light: void and darkness. And, in the beginning is the presence and movement of the Creator God: a wind, a breath that stirs the deep waters. From the very beginning the Bible holds together truths that seem to be in opposition to one another. The paradoxes continue: slaves in Egypt become a chosen people; the God on whom all depend enters the human story as a vulnerable baby; the death of Jesus becomes the breakthrough of everlasting life. Given this pattern, is it so surprising that hope is at home in unpromising places?

Most of us will be familiar with the experience of darkness and void: places and times that seem to lack meaning or purpose. The plan we formed for our future falls apart. The self, shaped by childhood experience, no longer corresponds with the self that now presses to emerge. The relationship we built our life around disintegrates. The work that gave us meaning and identity is taken away from us. The present seems formless and dark. Beyond our personal circumstances we gaze as people are torn apart by conflict or injustice, or worn down by poverty. Where is hope here? 'Here' is where hope is, for the Spirit of God moves over these dark waters.

Darkness and void seem unlikely companions of hope. Yet the dark of earth is where a seed begins its journey into life. The dark of the womb is where we all began: here we were nurtured and our individual features began to form. Once born, we spend half our span of life in the night; there we find the physical and mental rest on which our well-being depends. The Church's first celebration of Easter finds home in the dark of Holy Saturday night; there, as light gathers, we hear the story of our salvation. Darkness reveals the beauty of the stars; we are mesmerized by the flame of candle and fire in its midst. The void, too, might seem an unlikely dwelling place for hope. The busy, frenetic and noisy time in which we live works in every way to hold back emptiness. But what do we miss: the quiet in which to hear the deep stirrings of the universe; the space that untethers us from expectations; the room for what is true to be known? What would morning be without the night? What is a void but a place that waits to be filled?

All of this is not to deny the pain and confusion of being thrust into a place we did not choose, or how lost we can feel when we are no longer in control. The disorientation is real. And yet this uncomfortable 'here' and 'now' is also the first moment of creation, when formless void and darkness cover the face of the deep, and a wind from God sweeps over the face of the waters. Every moment and every place are held in this beginning. Here is the experience of the slaves in Egypt and now is when the bush burns in the wilderness summoning Moses to set the people free. This is the moment of the birth of Jesus, and this is the moment of his death and of his rising; and this is where you are now, reading these lines. The name of God as given to Moses is I AM (Exodus 3.14); and here – in the midst of our messy struggle of existence – God chooses to be.

Whether listening to other people as they tell their story, or being faced afresh with my own struggles and fears, I meet once more the darkness of helplessness, the loneliness of the void and the formlessness of unknowing. And whether or not

I feel it in the moment, I also know that the Creator God is moving over these dark waters. The book of Genesis tells of stars, sun and moon emerging from the shadows, and then of land, sea and sky and the life they come to hold. What will the next verses of your book reveal?

For reflection and action

Let where you are and how you are rest in God. Let go of trying to fix it. This too, as you give God room, becomes a creation moment. Imagine the breath of God sweeping over the dark water of this place.

8

God 'out there' or God 'here and now'?

When you pass through the waters, I will be with you.
(Isaiah 43.2)

For some years I used to run past a church that specialized in gloomy posters. One week it would be, 'Your sin shall find you out'; another, 'The wages of sin are death'; and yet another, 'Repent or you shall perish'. I wasn't tempted to join one of their services. My own church upbringing was for the most part less threatening, though I do remember the sermon of an outwardly mild-mannered priest who warned us that, because of our sin, we were dangling in a spider's web over the pit of hell.

There are many versions of 'God out there' that are less punitive. What they have in common is distance. 'God out there' is far away, waiting for us to get our act together and when we do, a relationship can begin. 'God out there' might be more loving and forgiving than the all-seeing tyrant of the worst of religious posters, but this God still requires a good level of performance to earn or keep our place. Even in traditions that have a healthy regard for the necessity of grace and the role of the Spirit in living a godly life, there can be an underside that suggests that individual competence, commitment and conformity are essential if any kind of relationship with God is to be maintained. Faith needs to be strong; doubt doesn't have a place. If you want to belong then overcome – or at least hide away – anything that doesn't fit the picture of a good Christian. The difficulty with all this is that we are left

GOD 'OUT THERE' OR GOD 'HERE AND NOW'?

with our awkward truth: often doubting, sometimes grumpy, tangled up in our conflicting desires; creative, kind and lovely in season, but beset with inconsistency and baffled by our inability to do better.

But what if the perspective shifts? Imagine that instead of 'God out there' we had God alongside us, where and how we are. Rather than waiting at a distance for us to resolve our inadequacies and overcome our challenges, this God looks out on life with us. Together we view the obstacles and work out a way of moving beyond them. We go together, rather than apart. Relationship with God is not the prize of the journey but the means of stepping out on it. Imagine intercessory prayer in this way. Rather than looking out or up to a God beyond, see you and God, together, sharing one view. You are both gazing at this person or that situation that touches your heart *and* that moves the heart of God. Now, go a step further. God is not only alongside but within. The capacity to face this situation flows from God in you and you in God. Where do 'you' end and where does 'God' begin? At times the distinction seems obvious, but in other moments you are less sure where the division lies. Is it God or is it you who dares to step out of fear, or reach out to the need of another, or who senses which path to travel? A homily for Holy Saturday captures the experience of travelling together. The author imagines Christ descending to the underworld to deliver Adam and Eve, the representatives of all fallen humankind, from the shadow of death. He grasps Adam by the hand and cries:

> 'Awake O sleeper, and arise from the dead, and Christ shall give you light ...
> I am your God who for your sake became your son, who for you and your descendants now speak and command with authority those in prison, "Come forth", and those in darkness, "Have light", and those who sleep, "Rise".
> Awake sleeper, I have not made you to be held a prisoner of the underworld.
> Arise from the dead, I am the life of the dead.

Arise, you who are the work of my hands, fashioned in my image.

Rise; let us go from here; for you in me and I in you, together we are one undivided person.'[1]

How do these words spoken to Adam meet you, where you are? Do you sense within yourself the stirrings of hope, not only urging you to step into life but also giving you the courage to do so? God, we discover, is not distant but close; not demanding change but making change possible. Together we look out from the darkness and see the first glimmer of light. Together we step out to find where that light will lead us.

For reflection and action

- What understanding of God have you grown up with: 'out there' or alongside and within you? What difference does it make to you when you shift your perspective from one understanding to the other?
- Read the words from the Holy Saturday homily above. Hear them from the place where you are. Where does Christ desire to go with you?

---

[1] Part of an ancient homily for Holy Saturday, author unknown.

9

Resting in hope

You pray and hope grows, it moves forward. I would say that prayer opens the door to hope. Hope is there, but by my prayer I open the door. (Pope Francis)[1]

Prayer opens the door to hope. Jesus urged his disciples to enter their inner room and pray to the Father, the God of hope, already present in that place (Matthew 6.5–6). Prayer in this sense is rest in what is given. We don't have to batter down the walls; there is a door, and it is always open. Naming prayer as rest might seem passive; however, rest of this kind is not the end of work, rather it makes possible a new work, in and with the God of hope. There are people I care for and tasks I am involved with. I move into rest when, one by one, I let them go to God, and then rest my sense of responsibility for these people and tasks. Now, they and I are moving once more in the flow of the God of hope. There is work to be done and kindness to be shown, but in and with God, rather than from within the limits of my own resources.

The prayer of rest is surrender, though not that of the helpless captive, forced to yield to overwhelming force. This surrender is a chosen movement into an embrace. Imagine releasing the tension of holding yourself together by letting go into the arms of someone who loves you. Imagine the freedom of floating on your back on the waves of the sea, rather than thrashing out your arms for fear of drowning. The trust that surrender requires is a choice more than a feeling. There is vulnerability in this prayer of rest, but a vulnerability that opens the door to

---

[1] Pope Francis, Message for Vocations Sunday, 5 April 2024.

what is already given: the loving labour of God on our behalf. The surrender is mutual, for the God of hope chooses to rest in you. Through this togetherness, hope moves forward.

Funeral services make familiar the idea of eternal rest. The phrase might lead us to visualize the inert body of a dead loved one, or the final stilling of the ever-questing human spirit. Rest is the end. In Christian hope, death is the doorway to abundant life. I can't imagine how this will be, which is not the same as saying I do not believe it to be so. The prayer of rest and surrender in this life gives some taste of what is to come; we die to our anxious attachment to being in control; we rise into the wonder of interrelationship. This rest is movement. Our spirit is freed in this resting place where we are known and loved. We've been sitting on the side of the room watching other people dance; now we get up and let the beat of the music lead our feet. This is as true in this life as it is in eternal life; or, to put it another way, eternal life begins here in our resting and moving in the God of hope.

The prayer of rest leads us into an attitude or stance towards daily life that is not confined to times when we are consciously praying. How to begin? Words might help, but keep them simple. Rather than pile up petitions, rest what is on your mind with God. Be like those people who stripped the roof over where Jesus was teaching so they could lower their paralysed friend into his presence (Mark 2.1–12). Theirs was an action, rather than words. You can lower yourself down too, in all your incompleteness and complexity. You might find it helpful to rest your body; scrunch up your shoulders and then allow them to relax; tighten your fingers into fists, and then let them slowly uncurl. Breathe more deeply and slowly. Rest in the moment, moving from the business and busyness of the mind into your senses. Even our thoughts deserve a break now and then. Listen to the sounds around you, or let your gaze be gently held by something you can see. As you move through the day, make room for these moments of rest. And if at this time you are trying very hard to rest and not succeeding, rest that self that is working so industriously; what you seek is already given; you don't have to earn it. The door is open. Hope moved in a long time ago.

For reflection and action

Read the story of a paralysed man brought to Jesus for healing (Mark 2.1–12).

- Imagine lowering your cares and responsibilities, one by one, into Jesus' presence.
- Imagine you are the one being set down and rested in Jesus' home. Let go; this is the time to be receptive to God's work in and for you.

10

Treasures old and new

> Therefore every scribe who has been trained for the kingdom of heaven is like the master of a household who brings out of his treasure what is new and what is old. (Matthew 13.52)

I am grateful for the theology I have studied: the gift of receiving the distilled wisdom of generations about the nature and activity of God. I have sat in classrooms and read books, wrestling with the meaning and implications of what I was being taught. Like wrestling, I often found myself thrown to the floor in a heap of incomprehension. In part this reflects the tendency of some theologians to gather very long words together in one sentence. Then there is the love – as in any field of expertise – to speak in jargon, which makes perfect sense to those who daily use it and confusion for those who do not understand the terms. I remember having to write an essay about the nature of grace. I wrote several thousand words about different forms of grace (actual, sanctifying, prevenient and other categories now beyond my reach) without ever really grasping what this 'grace' stuff was. The problem was that no one had helped me make the connections between what I was studying and the realities of my daily experience. Grace remained in my mind a mysterious substance connected with God and necessary for me, if only I could get my mind around what it was that I was missing, and then work out how to get it. Yet, grace was all my experience – the generous giving and working of God that was, even in that moment, drawing me into relationship and enabling me to grow.

I wonder if it is the same in relation to the doctrines associated with the Incarnation, argued about through the early

Christian centuries and expressed within the creeds. The nature of the hypostatic union matters for understanding our own experience of God's presence and working, but it's so easy to get lost in the thickets of attempted definitions. Here is something to know for day-to-day living: God is not distant and aloof; God is always where we are, even within the frailty of our human condition. John's Gospel begins with the Word, who 'was with God' and 'was God', becoming flesh and living among us (John 3.1–3). Mathew's Gospel draws on the prophecy of Isaiah to express how the son born to Mary and Joseph was also 'Emmanuel', a name that means 'God is with us' (Matthew 1.23). Beyond the limits of time, God is *there*, where we are. There is no place of human experience that God does not choose to inhabit. The Jesus of the Gospels expresses within the limits of time and place what is true always and everywhere: we are never alone. We are never alone in experiencing doubt, ridicule or defeat. We are never alone in facing the challenges or opportunities that open up before us. This presence is always drawing us into being. In Jesus' dying and rising, all pains and losses are being encompassed; all pains and losses are being gathered from death to life. These things I begin to know in the dialogue between past theological enquiry and what is going on within my current experience. Understandings – old and new – are in conversation, informing one another.

There is so much more to say about the theology of the Incarnation than what is expressed here. John of the Cross wrote of the inexhaustible treasures that lie in Christ, like a mine incomparably wide and deep where 'every recess' reveals 'new veins with new riches everywhere'.[1] Every opening holds a vein of hope. In his poem, 'The Wreck of the Deutschland', Gerard Manley Hopkins described the Incarnation 'riding the

---

1 Kieran Kavanagh and Otilio Rodriguez, 1991, *The Collected Works of John of the Cross*, translated and introduced by Kieran Kavanagh and Otilio Rodriguez, revised edition, Washington DC: ICS Publications, 'Canticle' 37.4.

river',[2] flowing from one life into all lives. Maybe this liquid quality is why theological formulations, as important as they are, struggle to express the mysteries at the heart of the Incarnation and its dialogue with our experience. And perhaps this is also why the apparent limits within our current situation will continue to be transcended by hope. This is grace: God's free and eternal choice to be where we are and work for our good. This is grace: the transformation wrought by this presence, and the love through which we continue to be created.

For reflection and action

- When have you chosen to come alongside someone who was upset or struggling. What moved you to do so?
- Who put themselves out to support you when you needed help? What difference did this make?
- What windows do these memories open up for you about the significance of God's choice to be with you, wherever and however you are?

---

2 Gerard Manley Hopkins, 1918, 'The Wreck of the Deutschland', *Poems by Gerard Manley Hopkins*, London: Humphrey Milford.

11

Waiting

I wait for the LORD, my soul waits,
  and in his word I hope;
my soul waits for the Lord
  more than those who watch for the morning.
(Psalm 130.5–6)

Have you ever spent a sleepless night waiting for the morning to come? The hours are long; the gift of light welcomed more intensely when it arrives. Waiting belongs in the rhythms of the created world; nothing can force the sun to rise before its time or the tide of the sea to turn. Yet, we live in a fast world where waiting is met with impatience. Not many of us like to be in a queue. Internet providers promise ever faster speeds. Gaps are quickly filled with something else demanding our attention. Waiting is an affront to our assumptions about how the world would work if only we were running it! Waiting is a useless, disempowering waste of time. We are dependent on events outside our control and it's uncomfortable.

Waiting has more to offer us than frustration. The first season of the Church's year, Advent, places expectant and hopeful waiting at its centre. We follow the longing of generations of mothers and fathers as they wait for the arrival of their child; for Mary and Joseph the day will not be hurried. Placing Advent at the start of the year suggests that the stance of waiting is the foundation for all that will follow. The beginning is God's movement and not ours. The need for receptivity and responsiveness to what God is doing never goes away; here is the source of our hope for a fuller, fruitful life: 'I wait for the LORD, my soul waits, and in his word I hope.'

The formation of any deep relationship rests on our willingness to wait, for waiting, as we begin to accept its place, is the relinquishment of our desire to control, grab or manipulate. In so doing, we make a respectful, humble space for the other. Good listeners know they must wait … not fill in the gaps … allow silences that in their time give birth to words. One who waits with humble and loving attention provides a rare place of shelter. Prayer is a form of waiting: not our filling the space with words, but the holding of our attention towards God. An open door allows God access to our depths. Empty, open hands can be held or filled; relationship deepens, transformation takes place.

Waiting can be joyful and expectant; waiting can be painful; waiting belongs within our experience. We sometimes meet it as interruption to our agendas, but waiting is relational space, pregnant space, space where words that have been too deep to utter come to be. The slogans of our age urge us to move on, get over it, or get on with it. But what might be forming in the waiting room: a truer self, a purpose for your being, a change of direction? What might be lost if you hurry on?

The short days, lack of light and the loss of form of Advent in the northern hemisphere may heighten our awareness of what is unresolved in our life: the question that as yet has no answer; the undefined, not wholly understood longings of our heart; the experience from which we are still reeling. In a world of speed, where the illusion of personal control over events is emphasized, our lack of answer or absence of resolution can come hard. Advent encourages us to hold our nerve: to wait for what only time and gift can bring. The season schools us in moving from anxious and frenetic activity to the stillness of attention and receptivity.

There are those, of course, who wait for a living; we call them 'waiters'. While for many, being a waiter is a short-term, fill-in job, for others it is a proud profession. The waiter looks for what the diner needs; responding readily. Is this a parable about our waiting on God? Yes – in part. But it is also the story of the God who waits on us, seeking us out wherever and however we are, waiting attentively, humbly, without violence or any desire to impose. After all, Jesus tells his disciples, 'I am among you as one who serves' (Luke 22.27).

For reflection and action

- Where do you need to hold your nerve and wait for what is yet to be revealed?
- Ponder this phrase from Isaiah 30.18:

    Therefore the LORD waits to be gracious to you;
    therefore he will rise up to show mercy to you.

    What might God be waiting to give you? Is there a door for you to open so that grace and mercy can be received?

12

Let's hear it for uncertainty!

> For as the heavens are higher than the earth,
>   so are my ways higher than your ways
>   and my thoughts than your thoughts.
> (Isaiah 55.9)

'I don't know where I am going.' 'I don't know who I am.' 'I don't know if I am right.' 'I don't know the answer.' 'I don't know how it's going to turn out.' Here's someone who is really lost! Can we help them get back on track?

There is an assumption that uncertainty is a bad thing and nothing to aspire to. We live in a culture that prefers ready-made answers. If we don't know how to do something, there will be a video on YouTube. If we can't work out that last crossword clue then the internet will help. If we don't know where we are, we can rely on the satnav to find our way. All of which makes uncertainty ill-fitting and inconvenient; if we are tainted by it in some area of our life, we might see it as evidence of our own incompetence or unsuitability for the tasks at hand. We need to move on to hard answers, and quickly.

Yet so much is uncertain. No one can accurately predict the future; we do not know how many days of life are left to us. If we enter a relationship with another person, we cannot be sure how it will work out. And is certainty all that it is cut out to be? What if my certainties are less than truth? We know now that the world isn't flat, and that the Earth is not the centre of the universe around which all revolves. Old certainties have the habit of dying in the face of new evidence. Perhaps if I don't know who I am that's a good place to be. There is more to discover, more to explore.

LET'S HEAR IT FOR UNCERTAINTY!

I know the paths through the woods where I walk better than most people. I came to know these paths by walking them, not knowing where they would take me. If I do become lost, I often know where I am since it's likely I have been lost there before. Through walking into uncertainty my world has expanded. We are nervous of 'un' words: 'unsafe', 'unsettled', 'unsure', 'unresolved'. The terms suggest they are the negation of positive values. Is it always good to be settled? What if we have settled in the wrong place, or in an insufficient understanding of who we are? Is safety always good? We grow up and gain fresh confidence by daring what is beyond our current competence or understanding. Safety can be a very small and limiting space. To be unsure is also to be open to what *is*, rather than attempt to fit reality into boxes of our previous making. Do we think less of a seed because it is not yet a fully resolved plant?

Hope is always a movement into uncertainty; hope, if we trust it, can liberate us from a known that is oppressive and limiting. This is not to say that uncertainty is easy; we are likely to feel more vulnerable in the absence of knowledge and control. Yet vulnerability itself opens the way to move beyond borders and into relationship. This is 'love' territory and 'God' territory. We can only come close to another if we dare to let go of certainty and trust what is ours to them. It's not so very different from choosing to walk down an unfamiliar path. We won't get lost if we decide not to do it, but we will never discover where that path might lead us.

Am I advocating recklessness: another negative term? Our warning signs about possible danger are implanted in us for a reason. We do need to consider the possible dangers of any new step we make. Embracing uncertainty comes with its costs. Daring to trust the stirrings of the Spirit within our spirit may disturb what's been settled and make us more uncomfortable. Yet, we cannot always stay safe and certain – not if we want to move further towards where life and truth reside. So, let's hear it for uncertainty and all those other 'un' words. They have the surprising habit of releasing what has been held back too long.

Be an explorer of lands you are yet to travel and of truths that wait to be revealed.

For reflection and action

Consider these 'un' words and the questions they hold:

- Unsettled: have you settled in the wrong place?
- Unsafe: is it time to dare what you fear?
- Uncertain: are old assumptions proving less than true?
- Unsure: is it time to wait for clarity to emerge rather than cling to past securities?
- Unexplored: is this the time to walk a new path?

13

When there is no rain

I will make a way in the wilderness
and rivers in the desert.
(Isaiah 43.19)

Through the woods where I walk there winds a small stream. In autumn, after heavy rain, sediment turns its colour to a deep brown. Small waterfalls form where fallen branches lie across the stream's path. On the coldest days, the tumbling current is furnished with icicles. As the trees around it begin to green, the play of rushing water mingles with the sound of blackbirds and thrushes; wood anemones grace its leafy banks. When the stream is alive like this, I feel its delight. Its movement is purposeful. As summer gathers and the rain no longer falls, the stream becomes a trickle, then a few pools of still and muddy water, until they too soak down into the dry land and depart from view.

In the years of my walking, the stream has become 'she', not 'it'. I wish her 'good morning' and I thank her for the life she shares. The rush of her water wakes my own sense of hope and purpose. When the stream runs dry, I feel my spirit's longing for rain to refresh me. The fluctuations in the flow of the stream mirror my experience of hope as a feeling. There are times when I rejoice in the tangible flow of God's life in me. It bubbles up in wonder, excitement and a keen awareness of presence. Then come seasons when the riverbed is dry. I feel my weariness, my heavy step. I am daunted by the obstacles in front of me and the weight of my own being. I miss the immediacy of the Spirit's flow. It doesn't take much to upset my inner equilibrium. Sometimes small defeats or inconveniences eat into my confidence. I mislay the memory of how God has been with me, season upon season, creating new beginnings from unpromising places. When I feel put upon, or unjustly treated by the turning of events, it's as if I am gazing mournfully at the dry river bed, fearing that the rain has departed for good.

We do not always feel hopeful. The feeling of hope is not ours to possess. It is in our nature to be afflicted with doubt and fear in the face of what we cannot wholly control. There are seasons when events drive hope underground. In its absence, we may feel defeated, listless and alone. Yet, even when the stream is dry, she has not departed. Her form has carved the landscape: there are depths and shallows in her curving path. The shape and the direction of her flow are clear. I walk the dry stream's winding path and remember the purposeful movement of water that has been, and *will be*. The flow of the Spirit in my life has carved its deep channel. If the water seems to fail in season, the shape of creative hope holds firm. This is why my daily walk takes me so often to the stream. She expresses the faithful presence that has formed my inner landscape. I act myself into what – for the moment – I do not feel. I begin to accept where I am. I call off the inner critic that delights in diminishing me. I step out into where hope goes and I do so in trust that God steps out with me and in me in this movement.

There is liberation in accepting that hope will not always be felt. Our experience is often difficult. Attempting to keep up a perpetually cheery face will prove exhausting. In season, we will feel down and defeated. Hope is a larger and deeper movement than we can contain or control. Absence of feeling is not absence of hope's purposeful working for our good. In the moment we find ourselves unable to see or trust in hope's movement; yet, hope goes on moving. I find it helpful to keep hold of some reminders of how relationship with God has brought life to me. I can look back at a journal from an earlier time and notice how growth was taking place alongside the see-saw movement of my feelings. I can go back – physically, or in my imagination – to a place or time when healing was happening. I can walk down to the stream and enjoy her company. In a dry season she is shaped to receive the rain that will return. I can wait with her, even if, for now, that is all I can do.

For reflection and action

- Read Psalm 42. Notice the ebb and flow of the hope it expresses
- Draw a stream. Along its bank, write or draw words or pictures that remind you of seasons when you felt hope's stirring.

14

Turning 'buts' into 'ands'

The wolf shall live with the lamb,
   the leopard shall lie down with the kid,
the calf and the lion and the fatling together,
   and a little child shall lead them.
(Isaiah 11.6)

Some words affect our outlook in ways out of all proportion to their size. For example, take the word 'but'. It's a simple, everyday word linking together two strands of perception that run counter to each other. There are probably few days when we do not have resource to it as a way of expressing our sense of how things are. Listen to these statements and notice what that single syllable does:

'I had a good retreat that gave me a fresh sense of my path, *but* now I am back at work and facing reality.'
'It's sunny now, *but* it's going to be cold and rainy later.'
'I am looking forward to seeing my friends, *but* the journey back is going to take ages.'

What does the 'but' do? With its addition the second part of the sentence begins to overwhelm the first. 'Reality' threatens to suffocate the insights of a helpful retreat. The presence of warm sunshine is put in the shadows by the coming cold and rain. The day with friends carries with it the burden of the long trip back. What follows 'but' is as true as what precedes it, yet it also results in the distortion of what is true. We are no longer in the sunshine now falling upon us; we are already in the rain that is yet to come.

TURNING 'BUTS' INTO 'ANDS'

The use of 'but' in this way can also reveal the presence of oppressive and limiting fears that have long dogged our path. As hope rises and we begin to trust God, ourselves and the possibility of a more fruitful future, old doubters throw out their snares:

> 'Is this really possible for you?' What about all the obstacles in your way?'
> 'What will other people think?'
> 'What if you're kidding yourself?'
> 'Look at the mess you have made in the past. How is it going to be any different in the future?'
> 'Can you really trust what you can't be sure of? Isn't it better to stay with what you know?'

I have grown to be wary of the power of the little word 'but'; it easily slips into my sentences and, if I'm not careful, into my spirit. Instead of 'but' I am attempting to remember to say 'and':

> 'I had a good retreat that gave me a fresh sense of my path, *and* now I am back at work and facing reality.'
> 'It's sunny now, *and* it's going to be cold and rainy later.'
> 'I am looking forward to seeing my friends, *and* the journey back is going to take ages.'

'And' accepts the truth of both halves of the sentence without one invalidating the other. I can hold both things together. I do not have to cast aside the insights of my retreat because I now face the challenges of my work. I can enjoy the sun, and – who knows – I might find unexpected joy amid the cold and rain that will come later. I can relish being with my friends and leave the journey back to where the journey back belongs – in future time that is not this time. 'And' allows me to hold what seems to be in opposition together. I can be fearful and choose to trust. I can laugh and I can cry. I can more easily accept and live all things in their moment. Nor do I have to attempt to fix what lies in the 'but' end of my thinking. If I put all my attention into this, then the hope that leads me in the moment will be overwhelmed and seem to disappear. 'And' is where God is and where hope resides; for God is comfortable with this reality and I am not alone in meeting it.

I give attention to not falling into the way of my fearful 'buts'; and I do not always succeed. In my attempts to turn from 'but' to 'and' I believe I am responding to God, who dwells amid paradox and mystery, and labours for us so persistently and creatively. But my belief is ridden with unbelief. Inevitably that 'but' rises again, pointing to my inconsistency and the inconveniences that so easily daunt me. And I turn to God once more, and ...

For reflection and action

- Give attention to your own use of 'but'. If you notice it is having a negative impact in how you view an area of your life, or a choice you want to make, replace the 'but' with an 'and'.
- You may find it helpful to hold your two hands open as an expression of resting both parts of your reality in God.

15

Hope's fabric

Consider the ravens: they neither sow nor reap, they have neither storehouse nor barn, and yet God feeds them ... Consider the lilies, how they grow: they neither toil nor spin; yet I tell you, even Solomon in all his glory was not clothed like one of these. (Luke 12.24–27)

I am sitting on a grassy bank at the edge of a car park. It is a warm day and I am grateful for the shade of a coppiced hornbeam tree. I have time to waste (or is it to spend?) before meeting up with my wife. Alongside me a daisy opens its yellow eye to the sun. Speedwell flowers mirror the blue and white tones of the sky. A bee explores the grass at depth, scenting or seeing its way. I notice it is small, almost black, save for two pale lemon stripes. The earth feels cool to the touch. A fallen twig wears ochre clothes of lichen. Now a woodlouse noses a brown leaf from a previous summer. I notice an almost intact acorn and weigh it in my hand. Near it is a plant with hairy leaves; I don't know its name, not having been introduced; a loop of goosegrass stretches out to cleave to it. I look at my watch, but it's less interesting than this small patch of car park grass – hope's fabric – beyond the reach of the lawnmower. For here, life is revealing itself as simply being and becoming; doing its own thing and succeeding in the task.

A woman emerges from the nearby shop and peers in my direction, wondering what I am about. What am I about? The question is there, but must rest for a while, for now a blackbird above me is beginning midday prayer, and a large bee, purposeful in its bumbling, is weaving through the spring forest of green about me. A spider climbs the mountain slope of my legs and passes on to the rough plain of my hand. Something is happening. I have sat here long and still enough to become part of this little universe. On another day I would not even have seen it.

What am I about? I reflect that I would understand this more by sitting in such disregarded places and allowing this connectivity of being to teach me. My senses help me come to my senses: gazing at the life that also flows in me; hearing the heartbeat of all being and my being; tasting hope in the growth that surrounds me; scenting the dying and birthing of necessary seasons; touched by the wonder of individuality and community to which I too belong. So much that is vital and beautiful is present in a small patch of grass; why do I need to travel far to see the world when it is at my feet?

Maybe this is why Jesus taught in parables, for in being present he saw truth all about him: the seed in its growth and the leavened dough in its rising. Like the lilies of the field and the birds of the air, he fully inhabited a small patch of time and place within the span and story of the universe. There he weaved hope's fabric for us all to touch.

I feel better for sitting here: less driven and more earthed. I realize afresh that we are never alone; our companions are all about us. You and I have purpose, and we can do worse than pay attention to the bee and the woodlouse in their sensory wandering to inspire us, moment by moment, to seek and find it. We can let go our anxious toiling and spinning for what we lack, for what we need is within us, and growing, like the blue sky of a small speedwell flower that opens at the sun's gentle bidding. Sit for a while in one place and give it your attention – as if no other place and no other time existed – and you will find hope's fabric spread out for you.

For reflection and action

Make space today to be slow:

- Sit and gaze out of your window. Listen to the sounds of this place.
- Go into a garden or park and savour what is growing there.
- Walk with measured step, allowing your senses to receive what you pass through.
- Resist the urge to move on and do something 'important'. Eternity is here.

16

The creative gaze of God

God saw everything that he had made, and indeed, it was very good. (Genesis 1.31)

What do you see when you look in the mirror? Do you like what you see? One of the worst things about this digital age is the number of times we see our face on a screen in an online meeting or conversation. In these mirrors, I see reflected the visible cracks and lines of age. I am not as young as I used to be, and it shows. How we see ourselves is also more than our appreciation or otherwise of our physical appearance. We are also aware of what we perceive as our faults, inadequacies and shortcomings. We are often our own worst critics and judges.

The first of the creation stories in Genesis joins seeing, making and goodness: 'God saw everything that he had made, and indeed, it was very good.' Pause there. Here is a first truth to take in. God beholds us as good; very good. Julian of Norwich, writing in the fourteenth century, expressed this truth both negatively and positively: 'He does not despise the work of his hands, nor does he disdain to serve us ... we are, soul and body, clad and enclosed in the goodness of God.'[1] I have lingered long with those words, for disdain is an apt word for the sense of shame so many carry. For some, disdain has roots in how others have responded to them, or failed to respond. Disdain creeps into our self-regard through our

---

1 Edmund Colledge and James Walsh, 1978, *Julian of Norwich: Showings*, translated and introduced by Edmund Colledge and James Walsh, New Jersey: Paulist Press. Long Text 6, p. 186.

THE CREATIVE GAZE OF GOD

perceived or actual failings: our apparent inability to meet the expectations others have of us or we have of ourselves. Disdain erodes our capacity to trust who we are, love who we are, or have hope in who we are. Yet, disdain does not belong; it has no place in God, and therefore no place in truth. Let the words soak in a little deeper: God does not 'disdain to serve us'. In God's sight we are clothed in goodness. Who are you? Your mirror won't tell you. Those who have cast their judgement on you and found you wanting won't tell you. Your own inner critic won't tell you; but turn to face the gaze of God and you will begin to understand.

In the creation account in Genesis what comes first is the act of making, as if God stepped back after the work of creating, looked upon what had come into being and was delighted. However, the movement of God is beyond the horizons of time we are confined to live within. God's seeing, making and delighting are in one moment that is also every moment and this moment. Creation flows from God's gaze upon what is yet to be, that in God's time already is. Like the author of Genesis, we do not have the capacity to comprehend the mystery of God, whose being and activity transcend time. Therefore, this mystery of Love enters time in the person of Jesus, giving us a window through which to understand the creative, eternal gazing of God.

In the Gospels the gaze of Jesus begins a process of transformation. Take the call of Levi, a tax collector. Jesus was walking along, surrounded by a crowd and he 'saw Levi son of Alphaeus sitting at the tax booth' (Mark 2.13–14). Levi got up and followed him. That simple phrase 'saw Levi' is no incidental detail; his seeing the tax collector at the side of the road was the pivot point of Levi's life. Words alone were not enough to move him to act; it was being seen that convinced him to leave behind the financial security of the tax booth. While others in the Gospels looked down on tax collectors, sinners, Samaritans, nobodies, Jesus saw beyond the labels to the depths of the person; depths that were unfamiliar to the one who was looked upon. He saw the good inherent in a person's creation before it was outwardly visible, and this seeing began to release the gift of their being.

Prayer is a way of gazing at God and allowing yourself to be gazed upon by one who knows you and wants you to be. In his poem 'The Glance', George Herbert describes how the 'full-ey'd love' of God will one day 'look us out of pain'. There's much in us that needs to change. Jesus was not blind to the faults of those he saw and called to himself; but his gaze didn't stop there; he also saw the person whole, free, fully themselves, the work of God's hands; and that is what God sees and works for in you and in me, in time and beyond time, creating, gazing and delighting.

For reflection and action

- What do you see when you look in the mirror? What does God see?
- For your prayer today, simply rest under the gaze of God.

17

In the valley of dry bones

> The hand of the LORD came upon me, and he brought me out by the spirit of the LORD and set me down in the middle of a valley; it was full of bones. He led me all round them; there were very many lying in the valley, and they were very dry. (Ezekiel 37.1–2)

Have you ever opened a Bible at random looking for a word of comfort or inspiration? Maybe you tried everything else and decided it was worth giving it a go. You close your eyes, flick through and find yourself completely and utterly lost in the book of Ezekiel. After reading a few lines you begin to wonder, 'What is he going on about?' This is one of the hazards of entering into stories we do not know. Ezekiel was looking to make sense of his time, not ours; and there was much he had to make sense of. God had called Ezekiel to speak to people who had neither the heart nor the hope to receive his words: fellow exiles, deported from their homeland to Babylon. Worse than this, they had brought this disaster upon themselves by serving their own selfish interests and straying far from their God. Ezekiel's particular gift was imagination; he was a man of pictures as much as words. Travelling deep into his people's suffering and his own pain, God provided him with visions of future renewal.

One vision took him into a dry valley full of bones: memorials of lives now dead and gone. As he gazed on the litter of death, Ezekiel heard the despair of his people: 'Our bones are dried up, and our hope is lost; we are cut off completely' (Ezekiel 37.11). How many times had he heard words such as these or felt them rise within his own thoughts? But as he stayed with the image a question began to form: 'Can these dry bones live?' (Ezekiel 37.3).

There may be days when you are with Ezekiel in the valley of dry bones. You survey the dislocated fragments of the present moment: the challenges ahead of you, the questions you don't have an answer for, the needs of other people and of your own spirit you don't know how to meet, the untidiness of past history and its effects. Can these dry bones live? I write on such a day; if hope is not lost, it has at least been mislaid. I have closed the door on another room in the house where cardboard boxes with flatpack furniture await assembly. The challenge feels too close to larger areas of my life that do not seem to fit. Will I be able to make sense of the diagrams that serve as instructions? Will all the parts be there? Rather than open the boxes I go back to Ezekiel and imagine him wondering why God had led him to this valley of desolation. Was it so he could see how fragmented everything had become and how hopeless everything was? Can these bones live, seeing how dry and scattered they are? Reading on, I notice how, as Ezekiel stayed with the question, God led him to an answer: the bones could live through the gift of breath, for all wakes into life through the breathing of God's Spirit; and, more than this, God's desire *was* to breathe this breath upon these bones. Ezekiel pictured what would happen: how sinew, flesh and skin would clothe the dry bones and the dead would wake through the breathing of God.

Then I notice how Ezekiel is asked to be part of bringing about what his imagination sees: he must step into the vision and summon the breath of God: 'Come from the four winds, O breath, and breathe upon these slain, that they may live' (Ezekiel 37.9). Encouraged by Ezekiel, I step into the hope I struggle to feel. God is actively working to integrate and make whole what I see lying in pieces. I don't have to know how or when.

I wonder whether this is what is asked of us on those days when hope feels elusive and we live amid the ruins of our current circumstances or our difficult past: to step with Ezekiel into the enduring faithfulness of God to us, and the love that is always active on our behalf; to do whatever seems to belong to us in the moment to do, and to rest in God what lies beyond our control. Can these bones live? 'Yes,' Ezekiel tells us, 'that's why God led you into the valley, so that the hope you had mislaid could find you afresh.'

For reflection and action

- 'Can these dry bones live?' Where in your life do you experience a lack of pattern and cohesion? Go with Ezekiel into the valley, and let God meet you there.
- This might be the day for a jigsaw. As pieces fit together, a picture will begin to emerge.

18

Looking forward

> Write the vision; make it plain on tablets, so that a runner may read it. For there is still a vision for the appointed time … If it seems to tarry, wait for it; it will surely come, it will not delay. (Habakkuk 2.2–3)

When we 'look forward' we anticipate the joy, the fun and the gift of what is yet to be. Our imagination has already begun to move us there. Imagine you've set some time aside for a holiday. You have decided where you will go and scoured the internet for the best deal. Now and then, between work, you step in to where you will be in a month's time. You look up weather reports and places to see. Perhaps you begin to plan what you will take, given the activities you dream of filling your days with. In those moments of anticipation, it's as if your holiday has already started; your mood lifts; you buzz with excitement.

Humankind has such a wonderful capacity to imagine; from the place where we start from, we can picture a different reality and structure our efforts to make what we see become real. As March begins, I look at our four raised beds in the garden and visualize what crops will grow there this year. I prepare the soil and sow seeds. Imagination energizes and motivates. Whether all that is sown will survive the slugs, pigeons, wind, heat and rain is impossible to know, yet without imagination nothing would happen.

Imagination is closely related to vision. Vision is sight; a 'vision' sees what will be (or may be) in the future. The work of the biblical prophets is shaped by the visions they receive, foretelling what will come to pass. Yet these visions do not come from the imagination of the prophets alone; they spring from the patient work of attentiveness to God. Habakkuk describes how he stands at his watch-post, ready to receive the word of God (Habakkuk 2.1). Martin Luther King's vision of a renewed American society, where children would not be judged by the colour of their skin but by their character, came from long and prayerful wrestling with the injustice of his time. The source of vision makes a significant difference. Imagination can work destructively. Ruthless dictators have employed the powers of their imagination in the service of their desire to dominate and exploit the vulnerable. When we've just had a heated argument with someone, our imagination might lead us into elaborate fantasies of vengeance. Maybe we need to take that mental journey to release our fury, but we might judge that more harm than good will come from acting out what we have imagined.

How then does the capacity to look forward with imagination relate to hope? The Holy Spirit, the source of hope, can work through our imagination to help us look forward to a better future and motivate us to face the obstacles in our path with courage and persistence. Martin Luther King saw a world shaped in the image of God where all belong at the table. His imagination was 'inspired' – Spirit-breathed. This enabled him to face and work through the dreadful reality he, and his people, faced of systematic prejudice, violence and oppression. He went on stepping into the vision when those around him suggested it was useless to do so. It is also possible for imagination to lead us in an opposite direction, away from hope, if it is moved by fears or greed. Perhaps this is one reason why the Spiritual Exercises drawn up by Ignatius Loyola and his companions feature imaginative contemplation of gospel scenes. Through allowing our imagination to place us at the heart of an encounter with Jesus, we see revealed the different movements of our own spirit: those that are the workings of Spirit-breathed hope, and those that run counter to the Spirit. Ignatius suggests that when we are moved by the Spirit, we begin to trust God amid uncertainty and to look forward in hope to the wider horizons of life founded on being loved and loving. When our fears and needs hold sway, despair displaces hope; we become afflicted with anxiety and feel separated from God and from others. Imagination reveals the habitual inner movements that govern our outlook and behaviour.

Imagination is not to be followed without discernment. As a God-given capacity intrinsic to our humanity, it is not to be disowned. Perhaps we can offer this gift back to God, asking for the grace that our visualization be Spirit-breathed; and when we begin to trust that this is so, to follow where it leads us with courage of heart.

For reflection and action

- Today, notice the power of your imagination in shaping how you see different situations and how this influences your responses.
- Ask God to help you visualize a path from where you are now to the place you long to be.

19

Feeding the blackbirds

For in hope we were saved. Now hope that is seen is not hope. For who hopes for what is seen? But if we hope for what we do not see, we wait for it with patience. (Romans 8.24–25)

I have suggested that imagination can work as an ally of hope, awakening fresh energy and courage through the picturing of what might be. But what if there's no clear vision? Is it possible to engage with hope when we see no way forward, no way out? Paul argues that the very nature of hope is that it is unseen. Imagination has its limits; seeing what is possible is not the same as the realization of what is possible. Hope works with and through uncertainty. But if we have no idea – no mental representation – of how God is going to work with us to bring about a better good, how are we to cooperate with hope?

Picture someone who feels trapped by an overwhelming sense of shame – shame that has its source not in the wrong they did, but the love that was missing in their early years. They struggle to make close relationships, doubting how they can ever be good enough to be accepted, and fearful of further rejection. Intellectually, they can understand the notion of love; they may be able to feel it within themselves for other people; but a wall comes down when it comes to anyone, or any God, loving them, or perhaps even more powerfully, *liking* them. After all, a good person might love a bad person; but like them? It is unimaginable. I doubt that willpower will ever be sufficient to bring about the feeling of being loved. But what if that person decides to act as if what they longed for might be so? They begin to defy their imposed shame by honouring their worth in practical ways: eating healthier food and investing in activities that give them life. With this counter movement the door of hope opens. Feelings of shame are likely to recur, their roots being deep; but action has begun to loosen shame's grip.

As I write this, I reflect on my experience of feeding the blackbirds in our garden. They are there each morning on the lawn, awaiting their daily meal of an apple. I cut the apple in two, open the door and begin to step outside. The blackbirds take flight. I know this is how it works. I put the apple halves on the grass and close the door. After a minute or two the blackbirds are there, taking their fill of the fruit prepared for them.

Why do the blackbirds take flight? Don't they know I feed them? Don't they realize that when their young come, I will keep a wary eye out to protect them from the local cats? And still, when I open the door, they fly away. They have an inbuilt flight mechanism, triggered by movement, and built over generations to protect them from harm. I wish them only good, but they move away. In another moment I am standing still by our garden pond. A blackbird comes down to the water to take a drink. Then she begins to wash, using her wings to splash water over her. She comes right up to where I am – no more than a foot away. There she begins to preen her feathers with her beak and shake her wings dry. The closeness is all on her terms and I understand this. I must stay still and not disturb her. Refreshed and clean, she flies away in the time she chooses.

I recognize how, like the blackbirds, it is hard to trust. Yet God understands this is how it will be, for now at least. We are not yet free of fear. Some of us have known harm in our past, and learnt to be on the alert, and fly at the first hint of danger. Unsurprisingly, we hesitate to put too much trust in God when she draws near, or trust her when she invites us to let go and find rest. Yet God persists in putting out the apple, day upon day, and allows us to move away to where we feel more comfortable. Until a day comes when we dare to draw close, and the fear and the past harm begin to slip away.

I will go on putting out the apples without asking or expecting any more, delighting in their company when they choose to draw near. Could God be like this: so generous, patient and persistent? Is that other God of demand and fear a projection of all that is wounded and wounding in humankind? What might happen if we dared, in spite of our fears, to act as if it were so?

For reflection and action

Consider how you might act in the direction of hope, in defiance of what you feel.

20

Remaking our mind maps

> I will lead the blind
>   by a road they do not know,
> by paths they have not known
>   I will guide them.
> I will turn the darkness before them into light,
>   the rough places into level ground.
> These are the things I will do,
>   and I will not forsake them.
> (Isaiah 42.16)

I like maps; I continue to resist the lure of a satnav. I enjoy looking at a map and planning a journey. Walking in unfamiliar land I will take out my map and see where I have come from and what lies ahead. Though we speak of 'reading' a map, what they offer me are pictures more than words; I can take out a map of an area I once travelled through and visualize the landscape I moved through and the view I saw. Maps only work in relation to the area they cover. If we go beyond the margins of the map, we have no knowledge of where we are going. It's as if we are blind.

In our formative years we form mind maps. Through our experience we build up a picture of who we are, what's possible for us, how to be in relationships and what's safe. These maps are necessary and useful while we stay in the same place; but when we start to stray beyond the familiar landscape of our assumptions the maps no longer work. Our instinct might urge us to turn back to what we know and have a map for; it rarely feels good to be lost. But what if we feel hemmed in by the margins of our maps? What if something inside us longs to explore new lands? The work of the Holy Spirit in our spirit is to do just that: to draw us to explore the more of who we are and who God is; to disturb us out of what is familiar but limiting. Like a seed planted in the ground, we are not content to live within the bounds set for us; a shoot, a stem, a flower and a fruit press to be revealed.

John of the Cross wrote from the experience of travelling beyond the margins of the map. His involvement within the renewal of the Carmelite Order led to nine months of imprisonment in a dark cell by members of his own religious community. His familiar mind maps could not help him navigate the trauma he experienced. His assumptions about his own future were smashed. Who was he in this place of darkness, removed from the known rhythms and expectations of his former life? Who was the God who allowed all this to take place? There was no outward good to be seen in the circumstances of his arrest and confinement; yet, this unknowing became the womb of a new and deeper life in God. In the years after his eventual escape John went on to write about the need to move beyond previous bounds. New lands, he pointed out, could only be found by travelling unfamiliar paths.[1] The old maps would not work. This would be a journey by night, without clear sight of where one was going, and it would also be an inner awakening of what was dormant within. The process could be set in motion by a change in the landscape of events such as John experienced; but it could also begin in choosing to respond to deep inward longing for the truth, wholeness and freedom that we lack. We cannot settle where we are and live; the old maps have to go.

For John, reason on its own is an inadequate path finder. Reason is trapped within its familiar maps and needs faith as a guide for going beyond what is known. When we have no map, we need God to lead us. Trust is vulnerable but, as we choose it, the bond of relationship with God grows. The will, he believed, has to move from attachment to self-preservation

---

[1] *Dark Night of the Soul*, Book 2, 16.8.

as its fearful driver to relational love as its motive force. The memory – our capacity to form mind maps and our tendency to cling to them – has to make way for hope, the Spirit's continuing reconfiguring of our understanding of who we are, who God is, and what is possible for us. Our horizons are expanding and hope helps us form new mind maps to help us explore the unfamiliar land we are moving into. Useful as these are, we are not to get over-attached to them. Hope has further to go with us; all our maps are temporary.

Without a map in our hand, God will not forsake us. In the darkness of his prison cell John found a new guide, one that burned in his heart, drawing him to step out of inner confinement into the wideness of the love of God.[2] In making this same journey we will find our own inner spirit awakened and our wounds made whole.

For reflection and action

- How might the God of hope be remaking your mind maps? How are you invited to walk beyond the margins of the map you received through your upbringing?
- Go on a walk you have never made before. Explore an unfamiliar street or footpath.

---

2 A journey John describes in his poem *Dark Night of the Soul*.

21

The dearest freshness deep down things

And for all this, nature is never spent;
  There lives the dearest freshness deep down things;
And though the last lights off the black West went
  Oh, morning, at the brown brink eastward, springs –
Because the Holy Ghost over the bent
  World broods with warm breast and with ah! bright wings.
(Gerard Manley Hopkins)[1]

The third week of February: all around me I sense the turning point between winter and spring. Birdsong is louder; tree buds are beginning to green; under the grey-brown of leaf litter, the first shoots of bluebells begin to stir; the sun rises higher and its gift of light is stronger. Winter is more than a memory; more cold weather lies ahead, and many flowers I look for remain buried in the earth, their growth still hidden from view. Yet, spring is here, not so much removing winter as rising within and through it; the two seasons greeting one another as one fades and the other rises.

Hope rises in this way, not dispelling our familiar struggles but emerging within and through them. This way of seeing things feels consistent with my experience. I might have longed for the eradication of anxiety from my life or some final freedom from being driven by this need or that, but it hasn't happened as yet. My upbringing remains my upbringing; my

---

[1] Gerard Manley Hopkins, 1918, 'The world is charged with the grandeur of God', *Poems by Gerard Manley Hopkins*, London: Humphrey Milford.

character is familiarly my own. I have no way of jettisoning my past. Paul wrote of how, in Christ, we become a new creation (2 Corinthians 5.17); however, this doesn't mean starting from scratch. Something more wonderful and baffling takes place. The bud on the winter tree opens; a green shoot breaks through the debris of decaying leaves; a blackbird sings morning while the sky is still dark. Just as hope begins in life as it is, not some other idealized or preferred place, so hope begins in us as we are, scarred and scared, daunted and doubtful. This is the fruit of Incarnation, the Word made flesh within all that is our story and through all that we have become. Nothing will be discarded; all will be integrated. The dead and defeated body of Jesus becomes the body of resurrection, still bearing the wounds of all that he has travelled through, and yet free from the nails that bound him in one place.

Here, hope connects with humility. Humility has nothing to do with humiliation. It is, as its root suggests, to do with earthiness. I don't have to run or hide from who I am. I can allow this reality to rest in God's good ground, as earth rests in its winter season. Rest is God's beautiful invitation. I don't have to perform, pretend or put on my best face. I can let go of beating myself up for not being what I imagine I should be. I can set aside my attempts to fix myself. I can do all this since here, with God, I am known and loved, beyond my capacity to know or love myself. I don't even have to feel that this is how it is between God and me; I can just dare to act as if it were so. In the chapel of St Beuno's in North Wales there's a wooden carving of Jesus on the cross that draws my attention. His near naked body is bent; his arms are outstretched, like a tree in winter stripped of leaves. Gazing at that image, I sense the invitation to also be my naked self, and to let fall everything that I am holding, feeling and struggling with. Here is a shelter for fears and longings, and a resting place for all that I am responsible for. Sometimes there are words to express what I desire to rest; sometimes there are no words; I am understood and received and that is enough. Spring goes on rising within this humble place of winter rest. All humanity rises with that body laid in the tomb on the first Good Friday. The more of who we are in God continues to break through.

I live in the cusp of winter and spring, aware of how awkwardly my humanity can express itself and also how fruitfully. I am not complacent about the ways I can let myself be led by fear as much as love. I ask God to go on healing this in me. I desire to know how I can cooperate with movement towards a more generous expression of who I am discovering myself to be. And in all this I begin to understand that rest in God is where that never-spent freshness, deep down things, comes to be.

For reflection and action

Do you sense any signs of this 'dearest freshness deep down things' at work in you? Is there one way you can cooperate with this springtime in your spirit?

22

Hope and cooperation

I planted, Apollos watered, but God gave the growth.
(1 Corinthians 3.6)

Gardening teaches the art of cooperation. My own shift from being an aspiring gardener to someone whose fingers are often muddy from digging or planting took place when I dared to defy my ignorance, open a packet of seeds and (having read the instructions on the back) nestled them in soil. I was involved; but it wasn't, as I had feared, all down to me. The seeds had within them the desire to become. Over time I have learnt that being receptive and responsive holds the key. There are moments when seedlings need water, or potting on, and I do this, without running to the assumption that I am making them grow. Like the movement of hope within us, their development is of us and also beyond us. We are there to be attentive, to sense what is needed, and to respond.

I remember listening to Mendelssohn's *Songs without Words*. These are short piano pieces, shifting in their mood and tempo. One of the songs caught my attention: a heartbeat between each note; the melody soared upwards, then stepped away like the turning of a kestrel in the wind. The thought came: 'How did he know what note came next?' And the answer came: 'He didn't; the piano knew.' I'm not looking to take away any credit from Mendelssohn. He understood his craft. He knew that a melody couldn't be muscled out of the air by sheer force of mind. His stance was receptive: actively listening to what was forming, and allowing the intuitive movement of his fingers over the keys to reveal to him what came next. Artists of any kind come to know that they must be both receptive and responsive. Their work is their own, and it is also a mystery beyond their making.

This receptive–responsive stance is vital in developing the art of cooperation. An understanding of hope that relies on good fortune won't do; it leaves us entirely passive in the face of fate. Reliance on personal mastery to achieve our goals will fail to follow the rhythm of the creative Spirit. Hope is the flow of the Holy Spirit within – and *with* – our human spirit; it is always relational. We are involved, *and* we are not working alone.

Last week I played table tennis. The art of the game is being receptive and responsive: how is the ball coming to me and how will I send it back? There is freedom in the play, within the bounds of receiving and responding to the shots of the person on the other side of the net. As the game goes on, the players get better at anticipating what the other is doing. Although table tennis is competitive, it might give some sense of what cooperating with the movement of the Spirit looks and feels like. The choreography is based on attentiveness to what the other player is doing, and our suppleness of response. Through the experience of relationship, we learn to understand and move with the other.

In the culture of our time so much emphasis is placed on sole working and personal achievement. Effort and ability are all. It's down to us to make things happen. Paradoxically, we also live in a time when it's easy to feel a victim of large, impersonal forces that we are powerless to resist. Lacking the capacity to make a difference, the temptation is to fold our hands and allow events to take their course. Hope invites us to ditch both muscular achievement and helpless passivity. Our ground for a different response is relationship; from that ground we can be attentive, and we can be creative. Hope joins contemplation and action, receptivity and response, individuality and common life. Setting aside time to be present to God in prayer, and actively engaging with the needs of our time, are an integrated participation in the life of the Trinity. Together, we are shaped in the image of a relational God whose nature is to cooperate rather than impose. We need one another's insights, abilities and energy if we are to thrive. We need to work together. Collectively we have spent too much energy on being human-aggressive. It's time to discover who we are in God: humankind.

The composer's hands are poised over the piano. His mind and body are focused on the task, yet open to receive what comes as gift, so mysteriously. What will be the next note of the song?

For reflection and action

- Where do you experience this receptive–responsive relationship within daily life?
- Is there an area of your life where a shift from self-reliance to working cooperatively with the Spirit is needed?

23

Painting from your corner

> Ask, and it will be given to you; search, and you will find; knock, and the door will be opened for you. (Luke 11.9)

It was going so well. The small roller I had bought fitted the width of the floorboards perfectly. The paint applied evenly. I would finish the first coat on the kitchen floor in no time. I was almost there: one last corner to paint; the one I was now standing in. And then the realization that I had no way out, at least until the paint dried. How had I managed to paint myself into a corner?

Standing there with roller in my hand I thought about the last time I had used that phrase – metaphorically – in conversation with a friend. I was talking about job prospects and ways of earning a living. It seemed then that every choice I had made, or been made for me, had taken me into a narrower space of experience and expertise. I had always worked with church organizations. What use would anyone outside that sector have for me? Aged 50 and feeling the need for further resourcing I had chosen to study Christian spirituality rather than acquire a new skill deemed useful in the wider world. I was now approaching 60. I had given all I could within my current work, but I couldn't see anything beyond it. The reasonable voice in me counselled that I could stay in my current role until retirement age and then have the financial benefit of a larger pension coming in. But though there was much in my work that I cared about, I knew that some essential part of my spirit was eroding away. Limping along didn't seem a good option. I could see no good way out from where I had led myself. But then, a few days later, a new thought surfaced: 'If you have painted yourself into a corner, then paint from your corner.'

Though there was no immediate answer in terms of a plan of action or a clear opportunity to explore, that invitation to paint from my corner felt liberating. There was energy here, the beginning of unreasonable hope. When I examined what had taken me to the corner I now faced, I could see my own choices at work. I saw my own indecision, born of a lack of trust in what I had to offer. I recognized my exaggerated sense of responsibility as a bread-winner, despite my wife's encouragement to follow where my heart led. I saw how easy it had been for me to lose myself in the work at hand and ignore what was happening to me. What I also recognized was the lifelong sense of calling to support others on their journey with God and enable them to befriend and express their true selves. This too was what led me in the direction of the corner I now stood in. What if I went further into my corner rather than seek to escape it? What if I trusted what was within me? I left my employed work and the financial security it provided and set out on a path of becoming a freelance worker in the field of spirituality. I would paint from my corner.

Perhaps you have a sense of being in a corner with no obvious way out. It might be to do with work, or a relationship, or a commitment you have invested in for many years, but now feels unsustainable. Perhaps all of your life feels in a corner. How did you get there? Was it events beyond your control? Do you blame your own shortcomings? Was it your passion that led you along what you thought was a highway, but that turned out to be a cul-de-sac? Perhaps it was a mixture of all these things. There are some important things to know: hope begins in corners such as these. God inhabits dead ends. The Spirit wakes in our spirit when we see no way to go. Rather than escape your corner you might travel further into it. Perhaps there is a doorway there that would have been impossible to see had you not come so close to it. Perhaps your corner – Tardis like – is infinitely wider than you imagined. Are you here because what is original in you asks you to trust it, rather than shy away from owning who you are? Is there work for you to do here that only you can do? What is the path this corner now dares you to travel? Or maybe your corner invites you to wait a while until the paint is dry. With God, you can explore what drove you here. A corner is a good place to survey what has been, and what might be.

For reflection and action

Stand in the corner your own choices and the course of events outside your control have led you to.

- Ask for the gift of awareness of God alongside you here.
- Seek understanding of God's invitation to you in this place.
- Knock at any door you begin to see before you.

24

God says: 'Go and have fun'

This is not the sort of encouragement many people associate with the Christian God. From the outside people often imagine church life to be solemn and constrained; from the inside it can sometimes feel that way! From my own upbringing I picked up the sense that the more miserable you were the better God was pleased. But hear these words from Pope Francis:

> Far from being timid, morose, acerbic or melancholy, or putting on a dreary face, the saints are joyful and full of good humour. Though completely realistic, they radiate a positive and hopeful spirit. The Christian life is 'joy in the Holy Spirit' (Romans 14.17).
>
> Christian joy is usually accompanied by a sense of humour ... We can get so caught up in ourselves that we are unable to recognize God's gifts ... He wants us to be positive, grateful and uncomplicated.[1]

If I consider the life of Jesus and his disciples, I see it woven through with fun and laughter. Imagine all those adventures along the road, stories shared and unexpected happenings. When you are with people you love and trust, laughter is never far away. Threaded through the teachings we have received from Jesus we can begin to glimpse his quick eye and sharp wit. How can someone who sees the speck in their neighbour's eye not notice there is a log in their own (Matthew 7.3)? Who tears up a new garment to repair an old and tattered one (Luke

---

1 *Gaudete et exsultate*, 126–27.

5.36)? Jesus was a natural storyteller, and a keen observer of human behaviour. He used humour to stir his listeners out of set ways.

When we start to take ourselves less seriously and laugh at how ridiculous we can be, we also relax and become open to life. To laugh and to find joy is not a denial of struggle or pain; Jesus knew these experiences well enough too. Laughter and tears lie so close to one another. When we laugh deeply, we often find ourselves crying. The emotions stem from the same deep place. Through them both we find release. Nor is the capacity to be light-hearted an indication of not caring. The burden we let go of is the weight of trying to be perfect by ourselves. We have need of another who loves us in our inability. We can laugh with compassion at that part of us that continues to believe 'all rests on me'. We let go of our self-preoccupation and become open to the universe. Humour and humility are the best of friends.

Jesus did not say, 'I have come that you may be solemn'; his expressed desire is this: 'that my joy may be in you, and that your joy be complete' (John 15.11). Ponder those words, 'my joy and your joy'. Joy connects with our individual being; it bears your shape and flows from who you are. You meet your joy when you are unselfconsciously and naturally 'you', without constraint. In this joy, your anxious, judgemental self is put aside – there's no room for it. Perhaps it is when you are being creative, in whatever form this takes for you: cooking, gardening, or painting, whether walls or canvases. Joy is also relational; you find yourself caught up in the wonder of the music the wind makes in the trees or a bird in the branches; there is joy in wonder at the being of another, whether a flower, or a child, or a wave upon the sea in its breaking. You might, with Jesus, marvel at how a seed becomes a tree, or the way yeast leavens dough.

Joy is a sharing in the being and relating of God. A good place for knowing joy is the experience of having fun in company with others, where being and relating become a delight that is shared. When I am in a meeting that has become too intense, I sometimes wonder if it would help for us all to go outside and play a game of rounders. When we were young, we had our playtime; have we grown too old in spirit, too serious, through mistakenly believing we can now do without it? In Pope Francis' words, the saints 'radiate a positive and hopeful spirit. The Christian life is "joy in the Holy Spirit".' Joy and hope play together contentedly, and they invite us to join in.

For reflection and action

- What is the shape of your joy? When are you most relaxed, creative and uncomplicated? When is your spirit at play?
- Do something joyful and fun-filled today.

25

The heart in pilgrimage

> Prayer, the Church's Banquet, Angel's age,
>   God's breath in man returning to his birth,
>   The soul in paraphrase, heart in pilgrimage,
>   The Christian plummet, sounding heaven and earth.
> (George Herbert)[1]

When my father died my heart led me in walking. I wanted to meet him somewhere other than the cemetery: a place that held nothing that was shared between us during his lifetime. My steps led me to the Downs, the chalk hills where, as children, he would take us in the none-too-reliable car; where we ran down the steep hillsides into the valley below, daring everything, fearing nothing; free and alive. There, on a hilltop, I came to what felt like the right spot and made a small cairn of flints to mark his living imprint on my life.

That pilgrimage seemed more led by heart than head. Inner longing has its own sense of direction, separate from any intellectual understanding. The movement in our own depths has its compass. The heart goes on its pilgrimages leading us to the places we need to be. George Herbert's poem 'Prayer' looks through many windows on what it is to be with God or to be surprised by God's being with us: the breath of the Spirit of God within the human spirit drawing us back to our beginning in God; the depths of our soul gathered and expressed; the heart setting out on pilgrimage. What is deepest and truest in us – the mysteries of our being we have only begun to know

---

[1] George Herbert, 1961, 'Prayer', *Poems*, Oxford: Oxford University Press.

– is forever searching for its place of belonging and means of expression. We live with the illusion of living in a settled and defined place, but our soul is going on a different journey. One winter evening I heard the sound of geese far above me and looked upwards to witness their migration to a new homeland. I think about that moment when the stirring of the colony began: a shared restlessness gathering among them, the first beating of wings, and then up into the sky on their momentous journey. Hope wakes like this, summoning us into movement, stirring us to seek the more that our spirit senses, even though our mind fails to comprehend where this inner restlessness is leading us.

Yet more rain made me reluctant to go walking today. The line of least resistance is to look out of the window, decide it's better to stay in the warm and dry and put away my walking shoes. But then I remembered a day when I defied my inertia and set out into the wet. I was tired and stale in mind. I wanted something more than familiar streets and known paths. I walked as usual past the gasworks, through the playing fields, around the ever-growing housing estate. At some point I saw a footpath that I had never noticed before. Its beginning wasn't promising: a muddy, narrow track between wire fences. But then, going further, I found myself walking through a cathedral of tall trees, as if along an aisle between green pillars. Some part of me wanted to kneel down. Here was a holy place my mind had no previous knowledge of, yet my heart had set out on pilgrimage for. The mystery continued to unfold with my steps: now I was walking through fields of sheep and the sun was breaking through; now a cloud of shimmering dragonflies stirred the evening air; then a slow walk home, full of thanks and wonder.

Not every walk brings us cathedrals of the trees or dragonfly-light, but, at the very least, the landscape changes with our steps and surprise may wait for us around the corner. The heart may sense this before the mind finds reasons to stir from where we are sitting. Maybe we have lived too long within the limits of our received self-understanding. Perhaps we have defined what is possible for us and unwittingly disowned the potential we hold within. Maybe we have decided that we are powerless to change what grieves us through lack of trust in where that longing for change might lead us. In all things it helps to know that we are not alone; the Spirit of the God of hope stirs within our spirit. Like the gathered geese we feel the unrest that precedes and invites movement. The heart sets out on pilgrimage, not knowing the path it will travel or what will be discovered there. The road itself will be the teacher: our way, truth and life.

For reflection and action

- Listen to your restlessness. Listen to your longing. Listen to the energy quickening within you. Do you begin to sense the pilgrimage of your heart?
- Whatever the weather, go for a walk today and see what happens along the way.

26

Stepping into hope

> See, the siege-ramps have been cast up against the city to take it, and the city, faced with sword, famine, and pestilence, has been given into the hands of the Chaldeans who are fighting against it ... Yet you, O Lord God, have said to me, 'Buy the field for money and get witnesses.' (Jeremiah 32.24–25)

The prophet Jeremiah has gained a reputation for being overly pessimistic, so much so that his name has become a description for anyone who sees obstacles rather than opportunities. Yet, who wouldn't be downcast given the circumstances he had to deal with: preaching a message of repentance no one wanted to hear; imprisoned for daring to speak words from God that flew in the face of the powerful; trapped in a city under siege from a ruthless enemy? There are often good reasons why someone feels overwhelmed. What we see in Jeremiah is a very human face; he is well acquainted with struggle; he sometimes doubts himself and doubts his God. He is not so sure of his ground that we cannot relate to him. Of all the prophets, Jeremiah is the one we see wrestling with God, questioning not only his vocation but his very existence given the harshness of his treatment by those he is sent to serve. He, above all prophets, expresses the pain of watching his people suffer:

> Is there no balm in Gilead? Is there no physician there? Why then has the health of my poor people not been restored? O that my head were a spring of water, and my eyes a fountain of tears, so that I might weep day and night for the slain of my poor people! (Jeremiah 8.22—9.1)

STEPPING INTO HOPE

No one who has watched with compassion the harm visited on the people of Israel and Gaza could fail to be moved by Jeremiah's pain; who among us has not asked 'why?' and felt helpless and bewildered in the face of needless destruction? Who would buy property in Gaza now? Who among us can see a bright future there? Yet Jeremiah takes up the offer to buy his cousin's field in a doomed city, choosing to act on the word he received from God about a future he cannot see: 'Houses and fields and vineyards shall again be bought in this land' (Jeremiah 32.15). No words could ever equal Jeremiah's property investment as an expression of hope. Despite all appearances and in defiance of common sense, Jeremiah trusts that this is where the God of hope dwells: amid the ruined houses and the ravaged fields; with the displaced people who have no safe place to shelter. In stepping into the direction of hope he himself becomes hope for his generations and for generations beyond his knowing. He takes people with him to witness the step he has taken, knowing that many will take him for a fool.

Jeremiah's choice to act in defiance of current circumstances tells us that hope is not first and foremost a feeling. Hope is the creative movement of God within the place we are, however difficult it might be or how inadequate we feel. Feeling hopeless is not in itself a barrier to hope; for even when we see no way beyond the limits that appear to confine us, we can still choose to step into hope. Jeremiah was schooled in moving beyond the limits of his vision from his earliest days. As a young boy he heard God tell him that he had been singled out to be a prophet to the nations (Jeremiah 1.4–7). His first response was to tell God to go elsewhere, for he lacked the experience and knowledge to speak. Ultimately, he chose to lay aside his misgivings. In absence of his own sight, he stepped into what God saw. He would go on doing so, even when the siege ramps were set against the city walls.

For reflection and action

What might stepping into hope mean for you?

- Perhaps it is daring to say 'yes' to where your passion and experience lead you in defiance of familiar fears that advise you to remain on safe and known ground.
- Perhaps it is a practical movement into caring for yourself when everything you have learnt has told you that you must give yourself away in saving other lives.
- Perhaps it is saying 'no' to the fixed expectations of others and risking their disapproval.
- Perhaps it is following Jeremiah in buying a field in a place of ruin. Hope waits amid the rubble; are you the one to wake it into being?

27

Plodding on

Who would true valour see,
let him come hither;
one here will constant be,
come wind, come weather.
There's no discouragement
shall make him once relent
his first avowed intent
to be a pilgrim.
(John Bunyan)[1]

A pilgrimage begins with a mixture of excitement and apprehension, and then settles down into a steady rhythm of movement; something we might call 'plodding on'. It's less exciting than that first spurt of energy and more wearing of the muscles of body and the mind. 'Plod' is one of those onomatopoeic words; the sound expresses the experience; a heavy, solid, repetitive step. We are too far from where we started to contemplate turning back, and too far from where we are going to be buoyed by any sense of arrival. Plod, plod, plod; like those people a long way back in the queue to pay respect to the body of Queen Elizabeth, lying in state in Westminster Hall; slow walking through long night hours.

Perhaps in one area of your life or another, the excitement of setting out has settled into a sense of plodding: the new job you took up; the programme of study you started with such anticipation; the relationship you committed yourself to; the care responsibility you willingly took up without fully realizing

---

[1] John Bunyan, 1684, *The Pilgrim's Progress*.

the toil involved; the prayer practice that doesn't seem to bring you any great revelation or prevent you becoming distracted. There is an honourable and necessary place for plodding. Plodding is an expression of commitment; a determination to stay with a choice you have made and a direction you feel drawn to travel, come wind, come weather. It will often be the way that commitment deepens, and its fruit begins to form, just as a long physical journey will begin to wake up our awareness of muscles we didn't know we had, and then in time strengthen those muscles and enlarge what is possible for us.

Imagine, for example, you decide to take up the practice of receptive, contemplative prayer for 10 or 20 minutes each morning. It's not so much the amount of time you opt for, but staying with what you have decided; otherwise, you might flee at the first onset of boredom. The commitment helps you persist when your thoughts protest that you don't seem to be achieving that peaceful and centred calm you hoped for. Self-doubt may creep in: 'Maybe I am not cut out for this – it's useless – I'm useless.' But you stay with the uselessness of it all, like a bird sitting on its eggs in a nest, day after day, night after night. As you do so, you let go of one way of operating, where you get what you want by taking it with your hands, and grow accustomed to something new: making room for the working of God. Through this receptiveness, God will integrate what is scattered in you, and draw out your depths. It will take time. You will possibly not experience very much even when, out of sight, the eggs hatch and new life wakes.

There is a necessary place for keeping going and defying the inward messengers who tell you how foolish you are being, or how inadequate you are. Having said this, there are things to be mindful of when plodding on seems the order of the day. Plodding can begin to become as heavy and reluctant as it sounds, especially when we feel put upon by lack of progress, or the persistence of the obstacles we face. It helps to regularly renew our commitment and remind ourselves why we set out on this path. When the 'oughts', 'shoulds' and 'musts' begin to weigh heavily, choose the road again. 'No one', Jesus said, 'takes [my life] from me ... I lay it down of my own accord' (John 10.18). Remember and reconnect with that first avowed intent. Don't get stuck in unhappy martyrdom.

Plodding on can go with looking down gloomily at our feet and failing to notice the small delights all around us: the daily gifts that remind us we live in a world of relationship, within the kindness and generosity of God. Stop and look up and around; receive what is given in this moment. This is also the pilgrim way.

Plodding on can be courageous and necessary. It can also be a way we avoid another and deeper calling. Fear can turn us back when hope rests in continuing; and fear can keep us where we are when hope moves along another road. What joins the two together is fear. No wonder this word of God comes so often through Old and New Testaments: 'do not be afraid'. We are not alone; walking with us, across the generations, are other brave pilgrims, and the songs they sung.

For reflection and action

- Where do you need the pilgrim's resilience to keep on plodding?
- Is there any area of your life where it's time to stop plodding on and take the risk of setting out on a new path?

28

Pilgrims of Hope

> Look to the rock from which you were hewn,
>   and to the quarry from which you were dug.
> Look to Abraham your father
>   and to Sarah who bore you.
> (Isaiah 51.1–2)

Pope Francis has declared 2025 to be a Jubilee year with the theme 'Pilgrims of Hope'. The idea of Jubilee has biblical roots; every fiftieth year was to be a year of liberation for all the people of the land; debts were pardoned, those in need were provided for, slaves were freed; even the land itself was to be given rest from ploughing, sowing and reaping. For Pope Francis, these practical expressions of justice and mercy epitomize how hope is never static; it is always flowing to wherever it is most needed. His choice of theme for the Jubilee year reflects his belief that hope is the work of pilgrims, echoing the daring pilgrimage of the Incarnation, where God became one with our human frailty to free us from our bonds and heal our wounds.

The position of Pope Francis captures the paradox within how the Church understands and expresses itself. He stands at the epicentre of a vast and hierarchical organization, set in the stone of buildings and structures deemed necessary to sustain its life; and he also represents the long inheritance of being a pilgrim people that must travel light if it is to be on the move. The rock from which it is hewn is the pilgrim, Abraham, who travelled to a land he did not know, in response to the God he was only beginning to know. The first name given to the Church was 'the Way' (Acts 9.1–2), reflecting a new and shared common life that needed practical organization to support it, *and* a people on a journey; like those first disciples who responded to Jesus' call to follow him along the road, *and* in the pattern of their lives.

Right at the centre of the Church as institution, Pope Francis insists that its spirit must be that of a pilgrim. Rather than settling down and becoming preoccupied with the maintenance of its structures and authority, the Church has to be a 'field hospital', going out of itself to be present where people are struggling. He challenges the Church to place hospitality above insistence on perfection of thought or practice, and dialogue above monologue. After all, this is the nature of pilgrimage, where people travel the road together, dependent on one another's support and guidance. Pilgrims dare the vulnerability of being open to whatever might meet them on the way; a pilgrim Church has to stay dependent on the providence of God and the companionship of fellow travellers, rather than stay safe within the bounds of its own resources and the limits of what it can control. In settling down, or shutting out, we lose touch with hope, for hope is always on the move, and open to share the journey with all who travel the same road.

The paradoxes continue: to be pilgrims of hope, collectively, within a broken world, we need the stability of organization. So many expressions of hope rest on systems that are thought through and consistent: night shelters, food banks, listening schemes, drop-in centres, community gardens. Structures and strategies can be hope's ally, rather than hope's undoing. It takes planning and commitment to respond to developing needs. These initiatives are the work of pilgrims of hope. What angers you? What moves you? Is hope at work here in these uncomfortable feelings? Many initiatives begin in this way. What might you do – individually, together, or as a church – to bring about change? This will probably mean moving in a direction different from the current reality. You are a pilgrim of a better future rooted in respect for the other, justice and compassion. You can respond to a one-off and immediate need; hope begins here. But what if you see that this need is repeated and widespread? Is there some collective and sustained response that could make a difference? And what if – as you explore the root causes of the need – you see that some challenge of existing systems is required? Campaigning to raise awareness or change attitudes is also the movement of pilgrims of hope. To sustain these initiatives you will need organization, strategy and structures; hope considers practicalities, and honours the importance of detail.

The Body of Christ depends on solid bones and supple sinews moving together for a single good. For Pope Francis, it is the movement of hope, in the God of hope, that holds together the seemingly impossible tension between the Church as institution and the Church as pilgrim. The rock from which it is hewn is the traveller, Abraham; the quarry from which it is dug is Sarah, from whom a wholly new future was born.

For reflection and action

- Individually and together, we have settled responsibilities, and systems to serve them. We are also called to have the suppleness and responsiveness of pilgrims. Have you got the balance right?
- How will you join the pilgrimage of hope?

29

The crossroad

When it was noon, darkness came over the whole land until three in the afternoon. At three o'clock Jesus cried out with a loud voice ... 'My God, my God, why have you forsaken me?' ... Then Jesus gave a loud cry and breathed his last. (Mark 15.33-37)

Mark's account of Jesus' suffering and death is unrelentingly stark. There is nothing to alleviate the darkness of the hour and the inward pain of the man on the cross. Contrast this with John's Gospel where, along with the horror of how Jesus is treated, there are subtle indications of the larger picture taking place. John signs us to truths inaccessible to those who were present, but revealed to those who read his words in the light of the resurrection. John adds the detail of water flowing from Jesus' side, like the prophet Ezekiel's vision of life-giving water gushing out from the temple and greening the wilderness (Ezekiel 47.1-12). In the moment of death Jesus 'gave up his spirit', as if here was another Pentecost (John 19.30). The body of Jesus is laid in a garden, echoing Jesus' words of the grain of wheat that bears much fruit through its falling into the ground (John 19.41-42; 12.24). John doesn't shelter us from the brutality and injustice of what is taking place; yet he helps us see the irrepressible movement of life even here, where death is most present. Mark gives no refuge from the awful reality of this lonely and painful death. Those who watch wonder if Elijah will come down to save him, but there is no deliverance. Jesus dies speaking words of abandonment; no one answers his prayer.

Which of these two accounts best provides a doorway of hope when events thrust us into places of deep pain? My sense is that we need both. Whether our grief and bewilderment have their source in the meaningless violence people inflict on others, or come out of personal loss and confusion, the darkness of the moment has its own overwhelming presence. No explanation can dispel the hurt and disorientation. This is Good Friday and there is no room to imagine an Easter Day. The pain must be felt; there is no path from here – only 'here'. Reassurance is empty; attempts to move us on to some brighter 'elsewhere' only add to the anguish. Mark's Jesus is present for us in our suffering, without delivering us from it. Hope is not absent, but it is entirely silent. Here is the crucifix rather than the empty cross, and that is how it is. We can do no more than find a way to endure.

John helps us access the wide horizons of hope, reaching into each and every place through those arms stretched on the cross. Even if we cannot think or feel it in the moment, life-giving water is flowing in this wilderness; the creative breathing of God is entering our stricken spirit; the buried grain of our existence is waking in the hidden place of earth, beyond our view. It is dark, and this deepest of nights is moving towards a new morning.

There are times when people of compassion can only offer those who grieve their inability to find words, beyond the word of their presence. There will be moments when we cannot see, feel or imagine anything other than the loss that afflicts us or the confusion we stumble in. The starkness of Mark's account of the Passion attests the truth of such experiences. Good Friday is its own day, and it may be a long one. Hope, respectfully silent, is present within the void of meaning and path and comfort. The death is real and will not be wished or imagined away.

John brings death and resurrection together in one view. The unseen is made visible. His is the hand of an artist who, with a few brushstrokes, helps the eyes to perceive and the mind to understand. We are not abandoned. Hope is present and active here. In this ending we have our endless beginning. There is blood and water of birth within this place of death. Such a painting of the scene might be beyond the moment of its witnessing; there are colours, shapes and patterns within the mystery of experience that only become known through time and long pondering. And when they do, they hold us through the seasons when we can find nothing to hold on to. With Mark and John, we stand at the crossroad between pain and its healing, death and life, despair and hope.

For reflection and action

- Ponder Mark's account of Jesus forsaken on the cross, present for you in your place of pain.
- Ponder John's signs: flowing water, the seed buried in the garden and the breath that gives life. How are these present for you today?

30

The grain of wheat

Unless a grain of wheat falls into the earth and dies, it remains just a single grain; but if it dies, it bears much fruit. (John 12.24)

So many stories about seeds: the Sower, the seed that grows by night and by day, the mustard seed, the wheat and the weeds that grow up together, and now here: a single grain. I can only think that planting seeds was something Jesus was familiar with; for the worker of miracles, here was an everyday wonder. A single grain, the fruit of rain, sun and soil, falling into the deep of earth; dead to our view through the harsh winter weather. Hidden still, another journey begins; the seed's hard outer coat breaks; a shoot presses upwards towards the light; roots move downwards to provide anchorage and nutrients. Unimaginable treasures are revealed as the shoot emerges to meet the sun: leaves unfurl, a flower forms and then myriad grains ripen; and all from the fall of a single grain.

Sowing seeds is an adventure of hope. It schools us in unlikely truths: the size of what you sow will bear no resemblance to what will come; falling and dying can become a pathway to living; working must befriend waiting; what is hidden will one day be revealed. Still more wonderfully, this generosity of life can break through without any human intervention. Any bare soil is quickly covered with new growth, often from seeds that have waited season upon season to begin emerging.

It was at Passover that some Greeks came wanting to see Jesus. What picture did they have in their mind? The image that came to Jesus himself was of a single grain of wheat. The grain could cling to the plant that bore it; or it could let go, give itself, for the sake of the life it bore that could only be released by falling. In the image of their Creator, seeds carry this trajectory within themselves: they dare to fall, wait and break to set free the life they hold; they are shaped for sharing.

Sowing seeds today, I consider the choice between giving and withholding. Do I dare to write these words or do I fold the book away? Do I trust that who I am right now, and what I have to offer within the limits of my knowing is worth sharing, or do I avoid the vulnerability of self-revelation? I wonder how that choice plays out for you in this season of your life. Do you stay safe, or do you offer what is in you to those who might need it. Do you put aside the desire that arises within to do something to counter injustice, inequality or lack of care, or do you plant the seed of that desire in God and wait for how it grows in you and where it leads you? Do you let familiar expectations shape your life, or do you allow yourself to listen to the unsettling stirrings of a deeper, truer self in its emerging? Do you dare let go, in the absence of knowing what it is that you are letting go into? These are the wonderful, fearful, adventurous ways of hope. These are the ways of seeds that dwell for a while in the dark before their birthing.

Every autumn the wheat releases its grain to the earth and dies. Another springtime, and new wheat rises. Once we were children and explorers, stretching out into an ever-new world. Now we are older and more conscious of our finiteness; the time will come for our passing. The wheat bids us dare this life as best we can, going with the generosity and abundance with which it lets fall its grain.

For reflection and action

Imagine God has given you two seeds of hope.

- One is to plant in a barren area of your own life.

- One is to plant in a barren area of the life of your church, local community or wider society.

In prayer hold each seed in your hand, asking God to help you identify where this seed is most needed, how you will plant it, and what care it will need.

31

Comfort's root-room

> Soul, self; come, poor Jackself, I do advise
> You, jaded, let be; call off thoughts awhile
> Elsewhere; leave comfort root-room; let joy size
> At God knows when to God knows what; whose smile
> 's not wrung, see you; unforeseen times rather – as skies
> Betweenpie mountains – lights a lovely mile.
> (Gerard Manley Hopkins)[1]

Why can't we hold on to joy? Why – if Jesus is risen and all that thwarts us overcome – are we so beset by doubts and fears? Why is the feeling of hope so elusive? Is it God's lack or ours? Are faith, hope and love all they are cut out to be, seeing as our abiding in them is so fleeting?

It's a heavy load to have to bear so many questions. I am grateful for the way Gerard Manley Hopkins shares his own exhaustion and finds a way, with God's help, to be gentler with himself; or as he puts it within the same poem, 'to live to my sad self hereafter kind, charitable'. There comes a time to 'call off thoughts' and 'let be'. Underlying the struggle is our desire to be in control, rather than be in relationship. We want to have peace and joy as our possession, rather than the gift of God. We want to achieve our final integration and to put down all that undermines it. After all, that is the legend told of how things work in our world. It's not that we are wrong to want to be more at rest with ourselves and free from all that encumbers

---

[1] Gerard Manley Hopkins, 1918, 'My own heart let me have more pity on', *Poems by Gerard Manley Hopkins*, London: Humphrey Milford.

our day-to-day life. This is also God's desire for us. But our integration will not be 'wrung' by willpower and effort on their own. This is God's slow work in us that we learn over a lifetime to cooperate with. So it is that Hopkins tells himself to 'let be' and 'leave comfort root-room'. Our longing and our effort are good; and for the rest of what is lacking in us, we need rest. 'Take my yoke upon you,' Jesus says, 'and learn from me ... and you will find rest for your souls' (Matthew 11.27–30). The invitation is to work together, not alone; this is what makes the burden of bearing our own persistent inabilities lighter.

Hope rests and wakes within this cooperative relationship. When we go it alone, we run the danger of slipping into the quicksand of despair. As much as our orientation towards a life marked by faith, hope and love is necessary, our movement there has its source in the giving of God. When, as far as our own judgement goes, we appear not to be making progress, we are not to beat ourselves up. While there might be something to learn here, falling into unremitting self-blame becomes another way we tumble out of the place of relationship. Sometimes the answer is not to try yet harder, but to humbly come back to the place of our rest in God.

Our feelings are also not entirely in our own gift. Sometimes we wake from a restless night, full of remembered or unremembered dreams, with a heaviness we neither want nor cling to. During the day, unanticipated situations or chance remarks touch into the places of our fear and self-doubt. We might find ourselves responding badly when our heart's desire is to do just the opposite. We become aware that we have become deaf and blind to the beauty of our surroundings or the kindness of those close to us. It's good to reflect with God about the source of our feelings and the consequences of them; there is something to learn here. But beyond this we need to 'live to this sad self hereafter kind, charitable'. As we do so we are aligning ourselves afresh with God rather than making ourselves distant and separate. 'Come ... and rest,' Jesus says. We learn that we can't possess the good feelings we desire – joy, peace, contentment, hopefulness – but they will come 'unforeseen times' through the generosity of God. A moment is approaching when joy will 'size', grow, fill us with thanksgiving. And slowly we begin to understand that while these feelings come and go, the truths they express about our resting place in God, and the loving creativity of the Spirit, are travelling deeper and deeper within us.

For reflection and action

Today, let your struggles, questions and incompleteness rest in God. Leave comfort 'root-room'.

32

Breaking the rules

We played the flute for you, and you did not dance. (Matthew 11.17)

The movements of the waltz – or for that matter any dance that requires precision of step – continue to elude me. Charitably, my dancing style might be described as 'freestyle' or 'original'. For all this, when the music is playing my feet want to move; I hear the beat and my body follows it; not everyone applauds.

There are rules in many forms of dance and they matter. Once learnt they create their own freedom, while allowing a partner to join in without fear of injury. There is delight in watching dancers express themselves within the bounds of salsa, foxtrot or tango, and still more delight (I imagine) in being able to do so yourself. Rules provide agreed guidelines and enable people to live, work and dance together. Here I am writing, and this too is a form of dance, with sentences as steps, shaped by rules of appropriate punctuation. Rather than being an arbitrary curb on individual freedom of expression, punctuation serves clarity of meaning, so that the writer's words can be in dialogue with the experience of the reader. Rules used this way express our interdependence; they remind us that we have no life outside of relationship. Driving a car, we know to stop at a red traffic light and moderate our speed according to the local limit. We have laws covering the safe preparation of food for sale and established customs relating to forming orderly queues; we have to live with each other and agree on systems that are both fair and in the service of collective well-being. When we break such rules, we run the risk of creating friction or causing harm.

BREAKING THE RULES

For all this, we have an ambivalent relationship with rules. There comes a day when we defy the rules imposed by our parents as we grow up. We find ways to deviate from the precise requirements of school uniform. Breaking the rules is one way we explore our individuality in the face of expectations devised by others, or even the limits we have imposed on ourselves. There comes a day when the seed breaks through the protective hard coat that has shielded it from harm and the chick cracks the shell that has thus far been its home. It is time to dare the life that is within us, pressing to be. Can you sense that movement in yourself, even now?

Sometimes rules deserve to be broken. Power can be used to exploit or subjugate others; systems of control can be deliberately or unintentionally oppressive, denying basic rights and freedom. Even religious law can work this way, as Jesus encountered in the criticism levelled at him for healing on the sabbath; rules are there to meet human need, not deny it. How could the scribes and pharisees insist on the tithe on cummin, mint and dill and neglect justice and mercy: straining out gnats and swallowing camels (Matthew 23.23–24)? To those in power, Jesus flouted the rules; but he himself declared that he had come not to abolish the law but to fulfil it (Matthew 5.17). Here then is something to ponder: freedom lies not so much in the abolition of boundaries as in the attention given to their purpose and placement. The considered formation of rules imbued with love of God, neighbour and self embody hope; they help create and sustain a place of common flourishing. The choice to seek and follow the way of justice and mercy is to move in step with the dance of God that Jesus leads us in.

For all this, Jesus was still perceived as a rule breaker, and in some sense he was. He sat and ate with the 'wrong people'. He created chaos in the temple marketplace by driving out the money-changers and overturning their tables. He told a provocative tale about an outsider – a Samaritan – who became a neighbour to a person in need while the established authorities walked by. He was condemned as a law breaker and died a criminal's death. He was dancing unfamiliar steps and those in authority felt threatened by it.

Jesus' nuanced approach to observance of the Law provides a way of understanding how defying the rules might turn out to be following the steps of a deeper, truer commandment. To our surprise, there come moments when hope urges us to disregard the assumptions that have thus far guarded our thought and behaviour. Our own internal authorities protest loudly, but the Spirit in our spirit will not cease stirring. Our feet are already moving to a different rhythm: salsa perhaps, or foxtrot, or something freestyle and original.

For reflection and action

- When has breaking the rules of previous assumptions or expectations proved liberating for you?
- Where is the dance of the Spirit in your spirit leading you?

33

Inclining the ear of the heart

Incline the ear of your heart ... What can be sweeter to us, dear ones, than this voice of the Lord inviting us?
(Rule of Saint Benedict)[1]

On and off I have a kept a journal for much of my adult life. When I say 'on and off' I mean just that. There have been times when I have written daily in my journal and felt it vital for my well-being to do so. And other times when the journal's only work has been acquiring dust as it rests in a drawer, unopened and unexplored. Many of us will have kept a diary at some stage. My university one coincided with the first time in my life when I was cooking for myself, and doing so on a budget. It was full of detail about what I ate, and often how disastrous it all was. I didn't keep the book; the recipes weren't enticing. I have a friend who can tell me (with a little research) exactly what he was doing on 23 February 1987, or 14 June 1998, for that matter. His diary (or diaries) are accurate daily records of events: where he went, who he was with, what the weather was like, and what was taking place in the wider world. As such – should I ever read them – they would be a fascinating insight into his life and times.

While a journal has many of the same qualities of a diary, it has a different focus and feel. A journal has a sense of dialogue. I am not just recording events of the day; I am in conversation with them. As I write, I explore my thoughts, feelings and reactions. It's as if the written page and the pen are asking me

---

[1] Leonard Doyle OblSB, translator, 1948, *Saint Benedict's Rule for Monasteries*, Collegeville: Order of Saint Benedict, 'Prologue'.

'What was going on for you there?' 'Why did that moment in particular feel significant?' I am not just talking on the page; I am also listening. As I write, the scattered fragments of the day begin to be gathered together. Patterns emerge; fresh insights glint in their light. Writing takes me on from where I started, to connect me with some deeper current within my own being, or with God's being. I am talking with myself and then I am talking with God; or to give the fuller picture, I am also listening to myself and also listening to God.

Keeping a journal enables listening, entering into dialogue, and becoming aware of God's transforming presence. The beat of the heart begins to change through attention to the scriptures of experience. Words on the page become a meeting place with God; a shelter to receive our deepest fears, hopes and desires.

So, how to begin? Many of us type on a keyboard rather than write with a pen or pencil. That's OK; but let what you write be for yourself and for God, rather than any other human consumption. Social media posts have a place, but not here. Or, go longhand. Buy a notebook and take out your pen or pencil. If you are wary of your own capacity to keep to commitments, start with agreeing with yourself to keep your journal for a single week. Then you can review how it's gone and begin again. You'll write about what is taking place in your life of course, but look to build in that deeper level of dialogue. Notice what you notice even if you are unsure what its significance might be. Perhaps each day will hold just one thing to give your attention to: what you heard someone say; a particular incident that affected you; something you saw. Explore your experience as the words go down on the page. Ponder your thoughts, feelings and responses in relation to what you have noticed. Talk with God through your words, and listen to what comes up in you as you do so. It may all feel scrappy, devoid of life-changing insights. Persist, and your receptivity will begin to grow. If you are not over fond of the written word, what about drawing what comes up in your mind? An image can express so much. Perhaps your journal becomes a scrapbook. Do you remember those? Images and words that express our experience are gathered in one place. They become more by being held together.

I have taken out my journal again. I know I need to pay attention. I see that I am more responsive to God when I do so. In monologue we never really escape ourselves, but dialogue leads us back to where God invites, and where hope leads.

For reflection and action

- Spend time reflecting on your experience of the day. Begin by remembering where you went, and what you did. Give attention to those moments when there was some inward reaction to what took place. Ask God to help you explore these moments and what they have to show you.
- Consider keeping a journal, as outlined in the reflection.

34

The basket in the reeds

> The woman conceived and bore a son ... When she could hide him no longer she got a papyrus basket for him, and plastered it with bitumen and pitch; she put the child in it and placed it among the reeds on the bank of the river. His sister stood at a distance, to see what would happen to him. (Exodus 2.2–4)

A fragile life exposed to danger: a Hebrew woman hides her child of three months among the reeds in the hope of saving him from death at the hand of Pharaoh; for Pharaoh has decreed that every boy born to a Hebrew must die. Moses – for this will be the boy's name – survives through the action of three women: the first is his mother; the second is Pharaoh's daughter, who finds the child and takes pity on him; the third is his sister, who carefully watches over him to see that he comes to no harm. Moses will go on to lead the people of his birth out of their slavery in Egypt. His name will be writ large in the story of the Hebrew people. Yet, there would be no Moses without the intervention of three women whose names we do not know. In their different ways the women defy the indifferent violence of their time. The mother hides her child from the fate ordained for him. Pharoah's daughter allows her heart to move her to act in direct contradiction to the edict of her father. Moses' sister uses her guile to persuade Pharoah's daughter that she can find a Hebrew woman to nurse the child, and so reunites him with his own birth mother.

How are we to measure the significance of the actions we take? Where will the story go beyond the choice we make to do something that is for life, rather than destruction? How are we to save the planet, end the violence and injustice, or create community rather than division? How are we going to change the situation of the homeless in our streets or the refugees who have no place to rest? Who are we to begin to put right the wrongs and harms on our own doorstep, within our own orbit of relationships? Who are we to think that our lives and our actions can make a difference? We can be overcome by the size of the obstacles before us. Yet, the path of life is not to measure but to do. In doing something – despite any feelings we have of the uselessness of what we are capable of – the God of hope begins to move. Imagine yourself placing a little child in a basket among the reeds. What have you set in motion? Imagine allowing your heart to be moved to show compassion to one you have been conditioned to think of as an enemy or a nobody? What change have you enabled? Imagine yourself watching over a situation with the readiness to say or do that something that brings good from a difficult place. How have you begun to turn harm towards healing?

It can be hard to trust in the significance of our actions. Perhaps we want to look too far forward: to see the whole thread of how what we do will be woven into a long-term difference. It doesn't seem to be the way things work. Even Moses, for all his endeavour, did not live to see his people settled in the Promised Land. He could only do what belonged to him to do, and do so moment by moment and step by step. The work of hope is mysterious, beyond our complete grasp; and it is always in motion, moving through this life and that life, this choice and that choice.

A mother hides her young boy in the reeds by the river; his sister watches over him. What if you are the child in the basket? Your very existence is the fruit of other lives. Along the way, others have watched over you and sheltered you from harm. Your presence in the world is meaningful, although you may not yet understand your meaning. You are meant to be. Others you do not know depend on the fruit of your actions. To you, God's hope is entrusted. You do not have to know the full picture. You will rarely be able to measure the good effects of the choices you make. Just do what you see needs doing, and let the story grow from there.

For reflection and action

- Whose actions shaped your life for good? Who made a choice to do something outwardly small for you that has had long-term significance? Bless those you remember, and give thanks for the fruit of what they did.
- Today, be open to any opportunity to serve another person's good, or to act in the direction of hope for our world.

35

The opposition to hope

> Not, I'll not, carrion comfort, Despair, not feast on thee;
> Not untwist – slack they may be – these last strands of man
> In me or, most weary, cry, *I can no more*. I can;
> Can something, hope, wish day come, not choose not to be.
> (Gerard Manley Hopkins)[1]

These are searing words; reading them, I feel the heat of the struggle from which they came. Moments, days, seasons such as these visited the priest and poet Gerard Manley Hopkins. Separation from familiar landscapes and friends, the drudgery of work he felt ill-equipped for, the discomfort of inhabiting his own skin, the silence of God when he needed warmth and comfort, all had their place in these dark nights and days. Strange, then, that in this poem I meet hope rather than the carrion comfort of despair. In the very act of naming his experience, Hopkins reaches beyond himself into the isolation of others who wrestle with an overwhelming sense of hopelessness. From the depths of his spirit, he summons up the defiant 'I can': the doing something of hope.

Within these reflections on hope it's important to honour the experience of despair. Few of us totally escape it; some, like Hopkins, live with it for prolonged periods. In despair we feel no comfort and see no way beyond where and how we are. Despair is not anything we wish on ourselves; we share no blame for it, though it often blames us. Considered as feelings, despair and hope are opposites. While hope energizes, despair

---

[1] Gerard Manley Hopkins, 1918, 'Carrion Comfort', *Poems by Gerard Manley Hopkins*, London: Humphrey Milford.

paralyses. Hope invites us into relationship; despair leaves us feeling separate and alone. The emotional experiences of hope and despair share this in common: they come and go, as all feelings do. Hopkins' 'can something' directs us to the doorway that has the capacity to sidestep the feeling of despair and its impacts: we can choose to act in the direction of remembered hope. Hope goes beyond feeling; it is an attitude, a stance and a movement that turns towards being rather than not being. There is a daring and difficult leap between 'I can no more' and 'I can'. Hope shows itself to be stubborn and defiant in the face of feelings and facts that seem to stand in the way of it. We can show kindness and compassion to ourselves in actions, when feelings insist that we don't deserve this. When the harsh weather of unanticipated events devastates what we worked so hard for, we can choose to begin again. We can pull out one brick of the wall that separates us from others by asking for help, or helping another. As we do so, we allow once-forgotten hope to gather anew in us, and we allow the God of hope to breathe fresh life into our spirit. Through a narrow doorway we emerge into a spacious room of possibility.

The psalmists knew the gift of allowing hope to move through their despair. Like Hopkins, they needed to acknowledge the reality of their feelings and talk them through:

> Why are you cast down, O my soul,
>   and why are you disquieted within me?
> Hope in God; for I shall again praise him,
>   my help and my God.
> (Psalm 42.11)

Despair has its day; yet, rather than feast on it, we can attempt to do something. Naming our disquiet is a beginning; remembering past blessing helps us shrug aside the heavy cloak of misery; acting in the direction of hope opens the door to a future we cannot yet see.

While despair is in many ways the opposite of hope, it need not stand in opposition to it. The true opposition to hope is

THE OPPOSITION TO HOPE

all that moves in the direction of 'not being': lack of kindness, injustice, destructiveness, exploitation of the vulnerable, the absence of respect for ourselves or others. We witness enough of these things in our world without adding to them. The God of hope desires to go with us along another way, marked by creativity, generosity, gentleness and the honouring of the created world and one another. We won't always feel so inclined; yet we can choose to be; we can do something.

For reflection and action

- How do you respond to these lines from Hopkins' poem? Do they resonate in some way with your experience?
- What is that 'something' that you can do today?

36

Hope and dialogue

I would like to enter into dialogue with all people about our common home. (Pope Francis)[1]

The opening words of Bob Dylan's 'All along the watchtower' have been going through my head: *There must be some way out of here.* There must be some way out of injustice and oppression. There must be some way out of humankind's casual misuse of the planet as nature drowns in a sea of plastic and the weather grows ever more extreme. How do we ever move away from the scandal of poverty and inequality; for all our technological advances, the gulf between 'haves' and 'have-nots' persists. There must be some way out of fake news and the love of power for its own sake. There must be some way out of greed and violence. There must be some way out of here. And then I reflect, if we are going to find our way out, we better understand how we got here in the first place. If we go on taking the same paths we will only go deeper into the mire.

In 2015 Pope Francis wrote an encyclical letter, *Laudato si'*, exploring the root causes of the climate emergency, the destruction of natural habitats and their impacts on the poor and vulnerable. He suggested that the recurring mistake humankind makes in tackling issues is that we do not see the connections. The different harms we inflict have a common root in our lack of respectful relationship with one another and with creation. We attempt to use power (technological innovations, physical force, financial muscle) to overcome successive

---

[1] Pope Francis, *Laudato si'*, 3.

crises that come up, while failing to see that it is the very misuse of power that does the damage.

The use of muscle is something churches themselves haven't been immune from. I remember in my early twenties going to St Peter's in Rome at the heart of the Vatican, and not liking it. My travelling companion, in no way religious, loved it. And I, a 'good Catholic', couldn't wait to get out. The vast building seemed to be an assertion of dominance. High, overbearing statues, gold leaf and mighty pulpits expressed unwavering certainties. Here was a place for truth to be asserted, not listened to. The opening line of *Laudato si'* reveals a very different tone: 'I would like to enter into dialogue with all people about our common home.' It's the opening line of a letter. It's also a man of power laying down his power, forsaking his boundaries, venturing out from his own house not only to teach but to learn; desiring not to enforce his will but to cooperate. He understands that this humility is the way of God.

There must be some way out of here. How did we get here in the first place? The challenge facing us, individually and collectively, is to turn away from mastery as the defining principle of our common life and to turn to relationships founded on humility and reverence for the other. This is the way of dialogue, and it is the shape of God's way of relating. In the way of mastery, we look for control. We are at the centre of our universe, and everyone and everything exists to meet our needs. We are acquisitive and possessive, insistent on claiming what is ours. Though this attitude has an outward appearance of strength and a tendency towards violence, what feeds and drives it is fear. We are on the defensive, against those who might challenge our supremacy. We like to build walls to shut out those not of our tribe: anyone who might challenge our way of thinking and perceiving. The way we communicate is by monologue. We tell people what is right; in other words, what we think.

In the way of reverence, we honour the other. We recognize our interdependence. We understand that we can only thrive by cooperation. Rather than hold what we have against the other, we express our common life by giving and receiving, according to what each one needs. The principle at the heart of our shared existence is love rather than fear. Rather than build walls, we welcome the other in, and go out of our own house to be welcomed by them. The way we communicate is by dialogue. Dialogue rests on openness: the willingness to listen to and learn from the other; an open mind rather than a closed mind. Dialogue is vulnerable and yet transformative. At the heart of dialogue is humility; we are stepping away from the royal throne and taking our place with everyone else as both servant and guest.

Perhaps this all seems abstract, faced as we are with very concrete issues that need addressing. But then dialogue is an activity, not just a theory. The open hand of dialogue has work to do. If we address the issues of our day through mastery and monologue, we only make more victims. Dialogue is not just talk; it is a willingness to listen, to look and to be moved to respond.

For reflection and action

- Where do you see the destructive impacts of mastery and monologue in current events?
- Look out for an opportunity today to practise the way of dialogue.

37

Hope has two beautiful daughters

Hope has two beautiful daughters. Their names are anger and courage: anger at the way things are, and courage to see that they do not remain the way they are.[1]

Can anger be beautiful? Can anger be aligned with hope and the God of hope? The more familiar associations with anger are violence and destruction: consider the ruination of Gaza, the storming of the US Capitol building, the assassination of dissidents who dared to defy totalitarian regimes, or the brutality of domestic violence. Nothing feels beautiful or hopeful here. No wonder that we are nervous of anger and often seek to contain it. I grew up fearing anger to such an extent that I disowned its presence within me. It took me many years to recognize that the denial of anger can also be a form of violence, though against oneself rather than others.

Like other emotions, anger simply *is*. That it exists as part of our human make-up suggests it has useful functions. Anger tells us when something is wrong. Anger gives us the courage to confront and overcome what is fearful. Anger rises when our needs are not being met. Having said this, unexamined anger can cause havoc. If 'something is wrong' is equal to 'things are not happening my way', or if 'our needs not being met' has its source in acquisitive possessiveness that shuts out any perception of the needs of others, then the energy of anger can be brutal and destructive. But anger can also serve life and flourishing, and in this sense be beautiful. An angry

---

[1] This quote has been attributed to various people, but its origin remains unclear.

Jesus confronted those who stood in the way of the healing of a man with a withered hand on the sabbath, since to do so, they interpreted, constituted work and therefore violated the Law (Mark 3.1–6). He went into the temple and overturned the tables of the money-changers, angry at their exploitation of the poor (Mark 11.15–17). This anger was *against* injustice and *for* the honour each person was due. On each of these occasions, the people he challenged began to plot against him. It takes courage to stand up to evil, and anger can help us take that risk.

The Spirit of God, the Spirit of hope, can stir within our human spirit in the form of anger. We are moved when we see violence visited on those who are most vulnerable, or the created world in all its beauty treated as an 'it' to be exploited or a receptacle for our rubbish. Absence of care bewilders and frustrates us. There is, however, work to be done in entering into dialogue with our anger. What is its source? What is being violated here? How can our anger be expressed creatively and responsibly rather than going down the cul-de-sac of blaming others and desiring vengeance? We do well not to disown rage; many initiatives that express justice and inclusion have their origin here.

There are also moments when the welling up of anger is vital for our own movement towards wholeness. When anything constricts us, we instinctively want to break free. Our learnt ways of behaviour become like ropes that tie us up if it is fear that forms the knots. Fear of what though? Fear of the person that is pressing to become from within, rather than the person formed by pressures from outside; fear of being rejected if we say 'yes' to our true and emerging self; fear of letting go of familiar boundaries even when they begin to take the shape of prison walls. Often enough, anger turns inwards, sapping life and joy; denying hope. But our God-given self is resilient, like a weed that finds a way to grow through concrete. If you recognize any of this, then receive your anger, rather than reject it. Perhaps it has come not to destroy you but to rescue you. Your survival instinct is showing what you might see as an ugly face; but has it come to reveal your beauty? Meet your anger with compassion; give it room to be heard and to tell its story. It takes humility and time to receive and begin to understand what is going on in our inner responses. We will need God's help to receive what our anger has to show us and to discern how to use this energy creatively. Hope is always beautiful in its working, even when anger is its source.

For reflection and action

- When has anger helped you overcome fear in a way that has been creative rather than destructive?
- Give attention to any feeling of anger you experience today. What does it show you about yourself, or what you care about? How does the God of hope invite you to respond?
- Find someone with whom you can safely explore your feelings, without feeling the pressure to conform to their expectations.

38

Swords into ploughshares

They shall beat their swords into ploughshares,
  and their spears into pruning hooks;
nation shall not lift up sword against nation,
  neither shall they learn war any more.
O house of Jacob,
  come, let us walk
  in the light of the LORD!
(Isaiah 2.4–5)

In the face of violence and destructiveness the prophets saw that the work and the materials that went into making swords could better be used to make ploughshares. It is not enough to hope in God and fold our hands until the bad becomes good. Hope rests on our cooperation with its flow. Someone has to begin melting down the metal and reshaping it, in defiance of the wisdom of the warmongers.

Rather than dispose of the metal it is reshaped; the metal itself is precious and useful; but we have to understand afresh what the 'use' within usefulness is. The distinction is made between destructive use (spears and swords) and creative use (ploughshares and pruning hooks). Rather than subdue or overcome our passions, desires and needs, the way of hope lies in discovering their creative potential. The effort to subdue, deny or root out anger, sexual longing, envy or any other feature of our inner being that might figure in a list of 'deadly sins' is likely to prove exhausting and fruitless. We are – in our wholeness – the work of God's hands. We are made in the image of the Creator God, so all we are has the potential to move creatively. The beginning is to own – even welcome

– those sides of ourselves we have learnt to feel shame about or to shun. Then we might reflect with God about how and why our needs and desires have turned in destructive directions, whether in relation to other people or towards ourselves. Then we can ask the Spirit of God to flow into and enliven these needs and desires so they take their true, free and creative shape. This is a lifetime's labour we undertake with the help of the God of hope. We cease to do war on ourselves or others, for hope's way is marked by reconciliation and integration.

Isaiah points to this new path: 'neither shall they learn war any more'. What we learn instead is dialogue. In the way of war, the other is a threat to our interests. They oppose us simply by being different and not under our control. The other must be subdued or cast out. This is the way of the clenched fist. The tight grip of our fingers expresses both violence and fear; we are ready for battle; we hold fast to what is 'ours' lest another should seek to take it from our grasp; we hide what is within. Our curled fingers are set against the possibility of relationship. We see these patterns played large in conflicts between different groups: the exclusion of outsiders; the oppression of those who do not conform; violence against the people of another tribe, nation or religion. In dialogue we begin to open up our hands. Tension is released. We are able to receive the other as they are rather than let them be defined by our fearful preconceptions. Trust can begin to grow and relationship to form. We become open to see difference as enriching rather than threatening; our uncurled hands can receive and give.

There are times when I am aware that I am going into an encounter with someone as if my hands are clenched. A previous meeting may not have been an easy one. I become aware I am wary, on the defensive, even ready for a fight. I have decided, often on little evidence, that I don't like them or they don't like me. I know that if I carry all this into the meeting then there be no real 'meeting'; we will remain apart and at odds with one another. I ask God to help me unclench my hands and release the fears I am holding. The other may not be ready to receive the openness I seek to bring; but often there is movement. Something creative, rather than destructive, is more likely to happen.

What we do in these small encounters – whether with a person or group we perceive to be a threat, or with those inner drives and needs we have hitherto despised or shunned – matters within the larger stage of relationships between nations and groups. We are either learning war or seeking dialogue. I wonder whether this is why I feel uneasy listening to prayers for peace in the world. Is it a way of keeping conflict distant from us? Is the true prayer to the God of hope to strive to let go of war in our own relationships, and so walk in the light of the Lord?

For reflection and action

How will you pray for peace in the world today by letting go of war in your own relationships?

39

The woman with two coins

Out of her poverty [she] has put in everything she had, all she had to live on. (Mark 12.44)

Sometimes hope expresses itself in actions that by the measure of everyday transactions seem unreasonable, but in the measure of relationship with the God of hope make perfect sense. What use is it, for example, to endanger your own life in trusting your all to God? Yet the calculation becomes different when you understand that the God of hope is the one and only source of that life you anxiously seek to preserve. Take the story of a woman who holds a sacred place within the Gospels for one action; placing two small coins as an offering in the temple treasury. She is the object of both Jesus' gaze and his teaching. Beyond this, her action informs Jesus' own choices in the days that follow.

The setting is the temple in Jerusalem. Jesus has travelled there with his disciples for the feast of Passover. The sun is quickly setting on his life. His enemies are already looking for a way to have him killed. Just a few days have passed since Jesus overturned the money-changers' tables. Now he is there again, sitting and watching as people put their offerings of money into the temple treasury. Some make their offerings quietly, without drawing attention to their actions. Others announce their generosity with flamboyant gestures and the noisy spilling of coin. There is little to draw the eye about a poor woman putting in two small copper coins. She doesn't linger. She's not looking for applause. Did she notice the man watching her? Her place is quickly taken by others; she merges back into the crowd gathered for the festival. But not before Jesus has called his disciples to give her their attention:

> Truly I tell you, this poor widow has put in more than all those who are contributing to the treasury. For all of them have contributed out of their abundance; but she out of her poverty has put in everything she had, all she had to live on. (Mark 12.43–44)

Everything she had ... all she had to live on. That will also be Jesus' way. She mirrored back to him the choice to give and not hold back. Perhaps, in a moment's faltering, she gave him fresh courage. It wasn't sensible, of course. What difference could her two small coins make? And how could one life, lived with courage towards the truth he sought to follow, heal the oppression, poverty and pain of the time that he lived in? But here was another way of accounting. What mattered was not an amount that could be numerically measured, but the desire this giving expressed. What the woman gave was 'all she had to live on' towards the God she believed in.

The more worldly wise among us might point out that the money she gave was likely to go in the pockets of men or towards vanity building projects, rather than to God. But that would be to misunderstand this moment in her life. This was more than a matter of coins; what she gave, using these tokens, was her trust. Her trust made her vulnerable; but it also opened her hands, mind and heart to the giving of God, who alone she had eyes for as she let go her offering. She might have kept something in store for tomorrow; but she wanted to hold nothing back from this trust in her provider, the one who gifted her life itself.

Isn't this the way relationships grow, when we choose to lower our defences and allow another to know a little more of who we are? Isn't this the way we grow when we take the risk of living out whatever is in us? When we let go of fear, along with our coins, status, what other people think of us – whatever our riches might be – we become free to do what is in our hearts. We also allow the other close: our lover, our friend, or our God. This widow chose to hold nothing back from this trust. She couldn't be sure what the outcome would be; but then this encounter was not about an outcome, but a relationship in which she rested her life.

The widow moves back into the crowd and out of our sight. But Jesus saw her then and held her in his memory. She might come back to our mind when we are weighing up whether to give or withhold, to fear or to trust, to live safely or to choose to be alive.

For reflection and action

- What is your unique offering? What is it you most deeply desire to share?
- Do something today that is generous – whether this concerns money, your time or your response to another person's need.

40

Easter hope wakes once more

> Why do you look for the living among the dead? He is not here, but has risen. (Luke 24.5)

Why is it that churches mark the 40 days of Lent with such vigour, and largely abandon the Easter season after one of its 50 days? Easter Day is a time of flowers, alleluias, colour and candle light, but that shared joy is rarely sustained and celebrated in the weeks that follow. Perhaps it's that joy is harder to hold on to than sorrow, and unshakeable trust more elusive than doubt. For most of us, struggle persists in one area of our life or another; the resurrection of Jesus has not removed our day-to-day difficulties. Watching the news, we see that the world is not fixed. Lent's challenge to find a new direction more readily accords with our spirit than savouring the experience of our liberation.

It doesn't help that some versions of Christianity seem to deny the reality that life can be difficult, we are sometimes difficult, and God can seem difficult! In this version of authentic faith, the resurrection of Jesus wipes away all uncertainty. Christ is risen and we have only to believe to live in a state of perpetual joy and tranquillity; doubt has no place and struggle suggests backsliding. But we do doubt and we do struggle. In this we are not alone. Keeping us company are the first witnesses of the resurrection. They too found Easter joy hard to hold on to; they struggled to recognize the presence of their risen Lord; they continued to know loss, confusion and fear. The Easter season helps us trace the surprise of hope as it breaks through the cracks of human frailty.

EASTER HOPE WAKES ONCE MORE

The resurrection appearances take place in the twilight zone between day and night, and faith and doubt. Mary Magdalene comes to the garden tomb in the early morning, while it is still dark. She is lost; even the body of her Lord has been taken away. In her grief she cannot see that he is right there, with her. It is only when he speaks her name that she knows the truth of what cannot be known. Though her heart is bursting with joy and relief, it is not a moment she can cling on to. She must leave the garden and go and find the disciples to share her impossible news (John 20.1–18).

Later that day, the disciples are gathered together in one room when they become aware of Jesus with them, even though they had locked the doors for fear of those who had put their Lord to death. Had he come through the locked doors or was he there all along? His first words are the greeting of peace: peace for their troubled minds and bitter memories. Jesus shows his wounds to his wounded friends and again wishes them peace. He breathes his Spirit into their failing spirits and gives them the capacity to forgive their own failings alongside those of others (John 20.19–23).

Then, we walk with two companions on the road from Jerusalem to Emmaus. Step by step they retell the story of the one they followed and the life he brought, only for everything to be lost. As they walk away from their hope, a stranger comes alongside. Their hearts begin to burn within as he gathers the fragments of their story and works them into a new and surprising pattern. It is only when the stranger breaks bread that they understand who has been walking with them. Even in the moment of recognition he is gone; yet that warmth within remains and hope now quickens their journey back to Jerusalem (Luke 24.13–35).

Simon Peter, who in fear has denied his association with Jesus, attempts to go back to the life that was his before he knew him. But failure greets him there too. There are no fish to be caught through a long, hard night. As morning breaks, a familiar voice invites him to cast out his net again. The size of the catch that follows overwhelms Simon Peter. He plunges into the sea to meet his lost Lord. I wonder if, as he arrives on the beach, his shame catches up with him. Does he hesitate then, unsure of how he will be received? Jesus keeps it simple. A welcoming fire is ready. 'Come and have breakfast,' he says. After a long night it's time to sit and eat (John 21.1–14).

These are glimpses, moments, neither looked for nor expected. The hope that wakes in these windows of recognition will not die, but the moments themselves cannot be held in their grasp. There will be difficulties and doubts again. Fears and failings will still arise. Life will not be trouble free. Mornings will still rise with uncertainties and evenings still fade with what is unresolved. But whether in a garden or a closed room, on a seashore or on a long road – wherever we find ourselves – hope will wait for us, walk with us, break bread for us, call us by our name.

For reflection and action

Be awake to how the risen Lord greets you today.

Afterword

May the God of hope fill you with all joy and peace in believing, so that you may abound with hope by the power of the Holy Spirit. (Romans 15.13)

I spent a good 20 years nervously edging around my desire to write. When courage and purpose finally came together, the book that emerged was called *Seeing in the Dark*, and its stated focus was suffering. At the time, I wondered about this sombre outcome of long germination. Was some gravitational pull at work in me, drawing me towards difficulty? My answer was 'yes'. Experience showed me that struggle and confusion were real and that few, if any, escaped some degree of suffering in the course of a lifetime. I was no exception. Yet the motive force within me in writing was to impart hope. For that was what I found moving in me through my work alongside people in hard places, and years on, hope continues to move me.

The theme of my second book, *Earthed in God*, was the nature of spiritual growth and the contrast between our familiar narrative of achievement through personal effort and ability and the biblical language of fruitfulness, where growth takes place through relationship. Through soil, sun and rain, seeds wake into being, providing shelter, food and shade for birds, bees and earth. We are not left to our own resources; there is life beyond us that we can cooperate with, and life within us that wants to be. There is hope.

The focus of my third book, *Send my Roots Rain,* was the spiritual welfare of priests, given the pressures they experience. It's been my privilege to be alongside many clergy, navigating their way through inward and outward expectations. How can they remain open to God's continuing interest in their own life and growth, and how might the very shape of their ministry create opportunities for receiving what they need for their own human flourishing? More than most, ministers need to receive the hope they seek to impart.

Perhaps the only thing I can write about is hope. If this is so, I am content. Hope has been my own warp and weft. I would be nothing without it.

The door of hope is open and God steps through it with purpose and compassion. Through this same door we can step out in God into all that is broken apart.

www.ingramcontent.com/pod-product-compliance
Lightning Source LLC
Chambersburg PA
CBHW060612080526
44585CB00013B/789